Reclaimed

Overcome Trauma and Gain
Healthy Control of Your Life

Shannon M. McGraw

Copyright © 2020 by Shannon M. McGraw

All rights reserved. This book or any portion thereof
may not be reproduced or used in any manner whatsoever
without the express written permission of the publisher
except for the use of brief quotations in articles and book
reviews.

Printed in the United States of America

First Printing, 2020

ISBN-13: 978-1-947637-02-3 print edition

ISBN-13: 978-1-947637-03-0 ebook edition

Published by DreamSculpt Books and Media

An imprint of:

Waterside Productions
2055 Oxford Ave
Cardiff, CA 92007
www.waterside.com

This book is dedicated to the adult women and men
who recognized what had been
done to them in the past
would no longer keep them in the darkness.
We are not victims.
We are not just survivors.
WE ARE THRIVERS!

table of contents

Note From The Author vii
Just So You Know ix
Remain In My Love by Patricia Budd xiii
Prologue: Letting Go And Letting God xv
Freedom by James xxi

Chapter One	What is Your Truth? What Are Your Facts?	1
	• Overwhelmed by Circumstance	
	• Grounded in Truth	
	• Focus on You: Self-Care	
Chapter Two	It's Time to Live	17
	• What Is Your Fear	
	• Create Positive Thinking	
	• Dream BIG	
Chapter Three	You Are the Key	35
	• You Aren't Broken	
	• In Trying We Succeed	
	• A.C.T.S. Prayer	

Chapter Four	Illuminate the Darkness	52
	• Lighter in the Light	
	• Creating Beauty from the Ugly	
	• Knowing Your Worth	
Chapter Five	Awake My Soul	61
	• No More Blame Game	
	• Be Confident	
	• You Are Good Enough	
Chapter Six	Claim Your Inner Wisdom	71
	• Don't Should've on Yourself	
	• You Have the Power	
	• What Do You Want	
Chapter Seven	You've Got This	83
	• Choice Is Yours	
	• Be Genuine	
	• Your Purpose	
Chapter Eight	Stand Firm	95
	• Who's Is in Control?	
	• Setting Healthy Boundaries	
	• The Gift of the SPIRIT	
Chapter Nine	Enjoy Life!	107
	• Do What You Love	
	• Celebrate Even the Small Successes	
	• Recognizing Daily Blessings	
Chapter Ten	Be Thankful	117
	• Forgiveness Heals	
	• Trusting Again	
	• Freedom	
Acknowledgments		125
About The Author		129

note from the author

Today is April 21, 2020, and I have been sheltering in place for the past thirty-five days due to the COVID-19 pandemic. A pandemic which has shoved the entire world into their homes, and thus impressively stopping the hustle and bustle of society. Taking away all temptations of frivolous living, explorative travel, and joyful gatherings or celebrations.

Many, like myself, chose to make a plan and gather as many family members as one house could hold to shelter in place—which makes the need for toilet paper dire. Unfortunately, others have had no other option but to be alone. In either scenario, our patience is tested and the hours in a given day become pregnant with unwanted thoughts, memories, as well emotions. For many of us, most had once been carefully tucked away.

At the point of the release of *Reclaimed*, the progress of freedom from the jail cells of this pandemic is slow. Therefore, I implore you to take this new normal of staying home to do some self-care, taking any negative effects of what transpired

Reclaimed

through the shelter in place to positive. Buy a new journal, or grab an empty notebook or notepad before beginning this journey. It is not necessary, however, from personal experience, I can attest to the healing qualities of writing out experiences and feelings. After each chapter is an opportunity for guided prompts, designed to help you explore your past and present on this healing journey.

Be intentional when coming out of this to be lighter in spirit, even if you are heavier in pounds. Your life is what you make it. It is up to you to find the blessings from your past, to acknowledge the hope for your future, and claim the joy that is yours today.

*Names have been changed to protect the identity and preserve the privacy of those mentioned in examples.

just so you know

In 2005, I spoke at World Youth Day in Sydney, Australia. World Youth Day is an event for young adults organized by the Catholic Church and initiated by Blessed Pope John Paul II in 1985. Coming home from my first experience speaking overseas, I was jet lagged and on a spiritual high. I couldn't go to sleep. A mantra was playing over and over in my head, and I didn't know where I had heard it, or why I kept hearing it now:

"Awake, O sleeper, arise from the dead and Christ will give you light."

When I got up to write it down, the mantra stopped and I fell into a peaceful sleep. The next day, I took out my Bible and, God as my witness, opened it up directly to the verse: Ephesians 5:14, "Awake, O sleeper, arise from the dead and Christ will give you light." I went to the beginning of the chapter and then read through to the end. It was Ephesians 5:6–20 which spoke my truth. My flesh covered in

Reclaimed

goosebumps. I didn't know then how the words on the page before me would resonate to become the inspiration for a healing nonprofit, or how it would reach women and men across the continents. I also didn't know how the words before me would become the blueprint to my own healing, as well the awakening of so many other voices.

The title of my first book, *Exposed*, was the first to manifest from these verses. Ironically, one year after publication, I found out the president of the publishing house was convicted of first-degree child rape. I got out of my contract with them and republished *Exposed* with a new cover— a true example of exposing what had been done in the darkness to the light. During this reprint, I founded Hopeful Hearts Ministry, a 501 (c)(3). It aides in the long-term recovery of adult survivors of abuse, through peer support and faith-based empowerment programs. I worked through it using these verses, to the best of my ability. You see, the healing journey is very unique to each individual. I do believe we are formed and given what's needed to heal in segments or steps within our life span.

In writing my second book, *Redeemed*, I had another dark, rather disturbing, and ugly truth puncture through to me. My layers of denial for survival had previously kept it at bay. This realization had been poking at me for some time. My grandfather had taken my innocence, at a very tender young age. The magnitude of this truth shook me to my core. Yet, at the same time it revealed my fullest truth. It allowed me to know *why* I often reacted and responded poorly, with no sense of true boundaries or direction, in certain areas of my life.

In knowing this truth, the real work could take place, so I no longer could claim a victim identity. Now, I was awake to so many areas of my life in which I had played a role with no authenticity, sincerity, or even genuine feelings. My marriage was the main facade. I knew what a good marriage was supposed to look like, and what a sacramental marriage should be within the eyes of the Catholic Church. Both he and I were not living our marriage out well. I tried to explain some of this in *Redeemed*, but I have to admit, when I wrote it, I was still in a place where I was struggling to fit the square edges of our marriage into the round hole of reality.

Before *Redeemed* was released, a truth was revealed which shook the axis of this facade. The ending of any seemingly good marriage or normal life can leave behind a mess of imploded dreams and memories, stacked like piles of rubble. We may question: *What had been real? What had been true?* But we eventually acknowledge that there had been no dignity. Nor any mutual respect. There was also little patience, kindness, or understanding in various aspects of our lives. *Was there love?* Yes. A love derived from care, comfort, and concern. Yet, it definitely *was not* the love of a good marital

Reclaimed

union, because it was defiled and discarded before, as well throughout, the marriage.

So, there I sat, a year after the divorce. Having gone through the blueprint from God, yet again, having given it over to Him, letting go of the reigns. I rummaged through the stacks of dirt and shame of my marriage to retrieve the heirlooms of what was good, because it was not all bad. In order to learn and grow, it is important to acknowledge the good and the bad. In the year since the divorce, one nugget I learned about myself, because of my abused past, was my addiction to chaos. Simply, it was familiar to me to bury what I couldn't acknowledge.

Now, the Lord has given me a new authentic relationship with myself in which there's a calmness like I've never experienced. I catch myself *trying to create chaos*, without even realizing it. Again, we subconsciously want to go back to what is familiar, even if it's unhealthy.

As God directs in this passage we are about to dissect, I am trying—truly working at it. I am setting healthy boundaries, exposing my "ugly," and trying to do the will of the Lord. In His will, God gives peace. Now let's get to work.

remain in my love
Patricia Budd

Remain in my love
But how lord you know my *woundedness* and misery

Remain in my love
Thru trauma thru abuse
I am always here at your side
I have not abandoned you

Remain in my love
Stay close by
Cling to my heart ♥
Be at my side

As the father has loved me so I love you
Don't forget that
I suffer with you
I am always with you

Reclaimed

Remain in my love
Don't search other ways
I am the way the truth and the light
I am mercy and love

Remain in my love
Don't seek the things
below in misery depression
But seek what is above

Remain in my love
I am here always
Let go in me
I'll set you free

Remain in my love
Give me your pain your suffering
Lay your head upon my heart ♥
Trust in me

Remain in me
Let go
and let me
If you truly want to be free

Remain in me
I am the vine
You are the branches
Stay with me

letting go and letting god

Done. I was done wanting control of an uncontrollable life. The only way I could be in control was to let go and let God.

Let go and let God. What a fun saying. So simple. So easy.

Not really. Not when you've spent your entire life trying to *be in control*. The irony of my life was with every struggle, stumble, and hiccup along my journey, I grabbed the reigns of control tighter, getting angrier and angrier at God for the life I was dealt.

"Nothing good ever happens to me," I'd say, both out loud and to myself.

"Why me?" became less of a question and more of a sarcastic, obligatory statement. I felt as if I *deserved* the struggles, stumbles, and falls. The older I got, the more cynical I became. The more cynical, the less interest I had in God, because surely God did not care about me.

If God didn't care about me, then it was doubtful I was *worth anyone's* love.

Reclaimed

Dysfunction. The number one component of dysfunction is the lack of living out the belief and knowledge of our worth; what we hold within ourselves, and the worth of those to whom we are closest. Jesus said, "Love your neighbor as yourself." Loving the neighbor is sometimes easier than loving ourselves. We know our deepest, darkest secrets and ugliest thoughts. The dysfunction derives from this need for approval, validation, acceptance, and understanding. For instance, a dysfunctional family is one that has varying degrees of chaos. Who you are and how you were brought up determines how much chaos, regardless of the type of chaos. So, what is often found is a group of individuals, *not a real* family. Each is different in personality, life experience, and self-esteem, which then leads to a battle over the control and desire, and who gets each of their needs filled.

I wasn't convinced God cared for me anymore, and I certainly didn't care for myself. If you showed me love and attention, I was yours. It was self-sabotage, but I didn't know it, and it took many, *too many*, years to come to this realization. Which was how, though now doubtful, I managed to fall into love with a man who lacked trust. Somewhere inside of me, my spirit cried out, longing for the comfort of what trust could give. Desperate to not be on guard, yet I craved the nourishment real love provided. The relationship became a vicious, ugly cycle. The stronger my grip on the reigns of control, the more muffled the voice of my spirit.

God was not hard of hearing, and despite my efforts to drown Him out, He stepped in and brought me to my knees, forcing me to shut up and look up. At first, I needed to acknowledge Him in my life. But eventually, *unfortunately*, the lies and the control began to creep back in. Then, God awakened my soul to His directive:

> Let no one deceive you with empty arguments, for because of these things the wrath of God is coming upon the disobedient. So do not be associated with them. For you were once darkness, but now you are light in the Lord. Live as children of light, for light produces every kind of goodness and righteousness and truth. Try to learn what is pleasing to the Lord. Take no part in the fruitless works of darkness; rather expose them, for it is shameful even to mention the things done by them in secret; but everything exposed by the light becomes visible, for everything that becomes visible is light. Therefore, it says: "Awake, O sleeper, and arise from the dead, and Christ will give you light.
>
> Watch carefully then how you live, not as foolish persons but as wise, making the most of the opportunity, because the days

are evil. Therefore, do not continue in ignorance, but try to understand what is the will of the Lord. And, do not get drunk on wine, in which lies debauchery, but be filled with the Spirit, addressing one another [in] psalms and hymns and spiritual songs, singing and playing to the Lord in your hearts, giving thanks always and for everything in the name of our Lord Jesus Christ to God the Father. (Eph. 5:6–20 NABRE)

There it was, step-by-step instructions on how to let go of the control, which controlled me and *not my life*. The answer to the question: "How do I let go and let God?"

A blueprint to freedom. Finding and dispelling the backhanded, passive aggressive, sometimes vicious arguments or actions, which subconsciously pulled your self-esteem and ability to know your worth into the depths of darkness. In other words, these were *empty arguments*.

This was a passage I referred to over and over again because I had come to learn that my journey was not perfected. Learned, but at times, I needed to go back to the blueprint to find my way. So, within this passage, I helped others change their directions, or let go of the reigns of control, to recognize their voices and know their worth.

Are you ready for a change of direction in your life? Do you feel out of control? Are you worn out

from trying to hang onto control, yet still getting nowhere?

Come along with me on a step-by-step, verse-by-verse journey into these passages in Ephesians. Give every step a shot. What do you have to lose?

Prayer to Begin

Blessed Father, I come to you in surrender. I am now letting go of the reigns. Please. Help me to see where You are in my life. And, to accept how important I am to You, and to others. Guide me out of self-pity, and my interior destructive behaviors, which keep me from true joy and happiness. With every passage in Ephesians, *please* give me courage to follow your instructions.

Through Jesus Christ I pray, amen.

freedom
by James, 43

Yellow butterflies
dancing in green fields
a young boy jumping
shouts of joy
and exultation

a wooden playhouse
a man
a mustache and glasses
words
that threaten death
if the secret is not kept

fear and terror
become compliance
the crushing weight
the wooden floor
pressing hard
against the boy's ribs

the silent cries
of pain, anguish,
submission

walking home
defeated
and bleeding
wounded
from battle lost

no rescue
no escape
only a secret

where was rescue?
where was father?
where was God?

Reclaimed

Weeping
she said

Weeping

for the little boy
for the man
for the evil

Later
wrapped in white towels
sleeping
atop the cold mountain
beneath the large stone cross

I love you
she whispers

I love you
my son

You are cradled
in my arms
comforted
by mother's touch

You are not alone
she says

I am with you

I will never leave you

I was there

God was there

Do not hate

but forgive

For it is in Mercy
that you will find life
and peace

the anger will destroy you
but forgiveness
will set you free

to live
and laugh
and love

again

one | what is your truth? what are your facts?

"Let no one deceive you with empty arguments."

Ephesians 5:6

It is safe to say, if you have picked up this book, you are either not happy with your life, or recognize maybe there is more—more blessings, more happiness and joy to tap into. Your circumstance might not be life-threatening or particularly dire, yet something has to give. Maybe you are feeling unsettled, or can't quite put your finger on what keeps you from feeling joy. Or you are in a less-than-ideal situation, which you don't know how to get out of. Either scenario leads to the same desires—freedom and happiness.

When just twenty-seven years old, I hated who I had become and wanted nothing more than to leave this world. I felt like an absolute failure—*never good enough*. To most, my life would have appeared perfect. Two kids, a husband who worked hard, we owned a house, had a golden retriever, and social plans on the calendar every weekend. But it wasn't enough.

I looked around and felt as if everybody else had more. Their husbands had the better paying jobs, or their houses were bigger, fashionably decorated with more character. If I set out to achieve a goal, I'd find someone else who achieved it faster. This, then, led me to feel as if I wasn't good enough to pursue the goal in the first place. Nothing went my way physically either. I had been diagnosed with rheumatoid arthritis (RA), I'd suffered a miscarriage, and two pregnancies of weight gain left behind fifteen pounds of unwanted fat. But what wrapped it all up with a complete dysfunctional bow was the molestation abuse from my grandfather as a child. As if not enough, two later date rapes in my teen years.

At twenty-seven, I certainly believed nothing good would ever come of my life. The anger with my life circumstances was so deeply seated, it surfaced as resentment, frustration, anxiety, and depression. My sex life suffered along with my marriage. Friendships waned after experiencing exposure to my wrath of disappointments and insecurity. The turning point came when my negative and pessimistic attitude began to affect my children.

Something had to give. Either I didn't want to live in this world anymore, or someone would have

to literally dive in and change me from the inside out. Obviously, I didn't know how.

God did just that, but in a slow process of steps. First, I had to acknowledge my facts, and then recognize what couldn't be changed. At that moment, these were my facts:

- Educated with a BA in journalism, and an MFA in humanities/creative writing.
- Married with two boys.
- Owned a house and two vehicles.
- Worked at home to be with the boys.
- Survived incest and rape.
- Suffered a miscarriage.
- Diagnosed with debilitating disease (RA).

What caused my discomfort and stress:

- Overweight.
- Depressed.
- Needed to feel in control.
- Filled with rage and anger.
- Cared what others thought.
- Strong desire to help others.
- Didn't like myself.
- Wanted to feel God loved me.

The fateful moment I came face-to-face with my ugly reality, I went into my bedroom, laid face down on the floor, and cried out to God. I knew as a child God loved me, but I had walked away from God as a teenager. I believed I had no other option but surrender, even if it felt as if He didn't like me very much. This was a huge step for me into trust. In the moment of surrender to God, I truly felt comfort. *He had me in His hands, and there was no need to worry about where I would end up.*

Of course, my life didn't suddenly become everything I longed for it to be. Next, I had to accept my facts, take a look at what caused the discomfort and stress, and then see what changes I could make.

- Exercise to help the weight gain and depression.
- Seek counseling to talk about the effects of the incest, rapes, miscarriage, and the RA. This would also work on the anger, resentment, and rage.
- *Find an outlet to help me help others.*
- Pray and learn more about God to figure out our relationship—attend a Bible study or a Mom's group.

These were tangible action items I *could* physically control. If I really wanted to see change in my life, to get out of the pit, then I had to put forth the effort. "God helps those who help themselves, right?"

"Let no one deceive you with empty arguments"

Ephesians 5:6

Know and understand, *empty arguments* have no truth or authenticity within them. They are words spoken to control you, and are *only opinions of others* who do not love or care about you.

So, where are you right now?

Do you live at home with your parents and feel as if there is no hope for independence?

Are you in a marriage which by all appearances is "normal," or at least "average," and should make you happy, but you can't ignore this feeling of discontent, frustration, or depression?

Do you feel trapped in your job or career? Does it feel as if it's a dead end?

Are you lonely and desperate for companionship and love?

Are you plagued by the thoughts that nothing good ever happens in your life? Is a negative approach your first response, and you only see the glass as half empty?

When we know God and feel God, we feel love, confidence, security, and support. When we are plagued with fears, insecurities, anxieties, and worries, *know* they are all led by lies of the enemy.

Who is the enemy? The enemy is the backhanded comments made. The passive aggressive cut-downs. The blatant disregard to healthy bound-

Reclaimed

aries. The snide and trite words meant to cut you down. The actions that harm or cause undo shame and guilt onto others.

The enemy encompasses and feeds on these empty arguments, which are intentional and purposeful. Meant to trip you up and keep you from being your true, unique, God-created self.

Let's write down your facts and decipher the "empty arguments" from the truth so we can continue to work.

For example: I worked with a young woman named Jennifer*. Jennifer was in her early twenties and about to graduate from college to begin a promising career in the field she had studied. She was well-known, liked by many, frequently attended church, and looked up to by both her peers and members of her faith community. When we met, she was the one "in charge," and by all outward appearances, seemed to have it all together with a promising future.

Except, Jennifer acknowledged that she felt trapped, unhappy, and hopeless. She admitted to having thoughts of suicide and knew she desperately needed help. One evening after I spoke to a college group at her local church, she waited to speak with me once everyone left. This was when she divulged the underlying source of her issue. "I don't think I'm worthy of having good things happen in my life," she said.

These words made my skin prick up with sorrow, as I carefully asked. "What makes you feel this way?"

"Growing up, my mom would tell me I was stupid and a whore. I would make her something, and she'd say it wasn't good enough. Then she'd make me do it again. She would laugh at me when my feelings were hurt, or if I cried. My dad would hear her call me names, and see her treat me this way, but he wouldn't say anything. I was in college before I realized it wasn't normal to have your mom make you feel like 'the dirt on the bottom of her shoe.' So, I asked my dad why he never stood up for me, and he told me he couldn't correct her in front of me."

I knew she needed counseling, which I suggested, as it would allow her to talk about all of these things her mother, and at times her father, did to her. They had left scars upon her self-esteem. These are her "empty arguments":

- You're stupid and a whore.
- You're not good enough.
- You can't do anything right.
- You're not allowed to show emotion.
- You're weak.
- No one is there to protect you.
- You're nothing more than dirt on the bottom of a shoe.
- You live in fear of your mom.

These empty arguments were deceiving her reality because they were false truths that caused

Reclaimed

her to feel less than human and not worthy of living. Talking about these to a professional could guide her into a healthier way of thinking about herself. These were key to give her the strength she needed to decipher and discern future empty arguments from the truth.

A few months later, Jennifer called and asked if we could meet. She had recently graduated and lived at home with her parents until her new job began in the fall. Outside of a coffee house, she appeared frazzled and stressed.

"What's going on?" I was concerned she was no better than the last time we'd met.

"Well, I was doing really well there for a while. I saw a therapist and it felt so good to talk about everything. But once I graduated, I've been living back at home and," her face contorted into a grimace, "it's so hard to be around my mother. She's worse now than ever. And, I don't know if I'll ever get away."

I realized I didn't have all the pieces of her puzzle, because I couldn't fathom what would make a grown woman stay at home with her parents when she had a job waiting for her in a town three hours away. "What do you mean you don't know if you can get away? You have a job. You are a grown woman about to make her own money and pay her own way. What keeps you at home?"

"My mother needs twenty-four-hour care," she admitted. "When I was in middle school, she had a medical condition that left her disabled. I've been taking care of her since I was eleven." The obligation was written all over her face.

"Who took care of her when you were away at school?"

"My father hired a nurse to do most of the work, but they'd made me drive home most weekends and sometimes during the week. I wouldn't mind if she weren't so abusive. Nothing I ever do to help is right, and there's moments I know she can do certain tasks herself, and yet she makes me do them for her and then screams, yells, and calls me names because I don't do them the way she wants."

"You've been doing this since you were eleven?"

She nodded, the crevices of despair and anxiety were etched deep into her young face. "I feel obligated because she is my mother. I mean I love her, but I don't like her. The things she calls me, or says to me are cruel. Most of the time I want to leave her where she is, and walk out."

Within my spirit, I prayed for guidance and direction. This was a touchy situation because of the obligation she felt toward her parents. *Obey your mother and father* was what kept her in this abusive situation. This was when I heard:

> Do not think that I have come to bring peace upon the earth. I have come to bring not peace but the sword. For I have come

Reclaimed

to set a man against his father, a daughter against her mother, and a daughter-in-law against her mother-in-law; and one's enemies will be those of his household. (Matthew 10:34–36)

To some it may seem crazy, but for Jennifer, I knew this pertained to her circumstance. With the full story, I realized her mother had narcissistic tendencies, and she not only wanted everything her way, but was jealous of her daughter. Narcissism is a personality disorder involving self-centered, arrogant thinking and behavior, and lack of empathy with no consideration for other people. Jennifer's mother's vile remarks to her daughter were truly debilitating and part of her narcissism, so not in any way connected to love.

Something we all have to be aware of from people we love. Jennifer's desire was to do as a daughter should, as God directs, to love her mother and make sure she was obedient. However, the chasm in this is when the parent takes advantage of God's directive and stifles the very plan He created for their child. At this point, Jennifer's parents were requesting she continue to travel the three-hour drive on weekends, and when needed during the week, even though she had a work obligation.

Forget having any sort of life outside of work and taking care of her mother who belittled, spat at, and pushed her around every chance given.

This scenario left Jennifer in a vice, which fueled the desire to *get out*, even if it meant taking her own life.

"What are your facts, Jennifer?"

She looked at me confused. "What do you mean?"

I found a scrap piece of paper and pen from my purse, then wrote out her facts:

- Twenty-three-years old—an adult.
- Full-time job/career beginning in a town three hours away from parents.
- Job requirement is 7:00 a.m. to 5:00 p.m.
- Sometimes extra work on weekends needed to prepare.
- Have a lease on an apartment.
- Mother is disabled.
- Father works and looks after mom at night.
- Parents *have insurance* to cover mom's in-home care.

Then we wrote down what caused her *discomfort* and *stress*: her *emotional responses*.

- Obligation to take care of her mother, because it's her mother.
- Desire to have friends and do things she enjoys, but hasn't had the time.
- The verbal and physical assaults of her mother.

Reclaimed

- The guilt—she does love her mother and father.

When she looked at her facts separately from her empty arguments, she was able to see a clearer picture of what control she was given. Her father and mother had made a commitment and covenant with one another to be there through sickness and health. She was under no such obligation to suffer through abuse, and lose sight of her own journey, in order to be a slave to her mother. If her mother were empathetic to Jennifer's situation, appreciative, loving, and acting in a merciful, Christ-like manner, the scenario would be different. Jennifer would have desired to find a job closer to her parents in order to take some of the burden from her father.

With her facts, Jennifer made a plan:

- Determined that day, she needed to move to her new permanent place of residence. Put space here?
- Determine the days she could be home in order to help with her mother—Holidays, possibly one weekend every six to eight weeks, or what her job allotted.
- Speak to her father about getting full-time care for her mother, and present him with the schedule she was able to adhere to in order to help.

Being aware of her mother's narcissism, and having a concrete plan, physically set Jennifer at ease. Once the plan was presented to her father, he had no means by which to dispute or argue her facts, or how she was willing to share in his burden. So, Jennifer was well on her way to discovering the journey God had intended for her. She felt totally free to explore who she was and how to overcome the years of verbal abuse that had left her so insecure. Now, when she was with her mother, she was prepared with the help and direction of her counselor, and so able to turn away from the lies and empty arguments.

Update: After a few years of this scenario in place, the relationship between Jennifer and her mother had slowly healed. Jennifer found when she went to help her mother, she realized her own heart to be more merciful. She instilled boundaries with her mother's verbal abuse, and followed through. Here are a few as an example:

- When you call me names or speak to me in a belligerent or condescending tone, *I will leave.*
- If you would like something done in a specific way, you need to let me know specifically, and ask in a kind manner.

Because Jennifer felt more secure and confident in who God created her to be, and in her self-worth, she was able to follow through with her boundaries. This led her mother to recognize she stood to lose any relationship she had with her daughter if she were not willing to begin working on *her own* internal frustrations, perhaps caused by the illness she suffered.

REFLECTION ON HEALING

What is a memory (or memories) from your past that continues to haunt you?

I spoke with a woman many years ago who struggled with her weight throughout her life. She wasn't a client due to trauma, she was merely confiding frustrations of her life and how she wanted to make a change. While walking her through these same steps, she immediately spoke of a memory that had plagued her for decades. She was a healthy, normal eighth grade girl hanging with her best friend. They went to buy a drink, and she asked for a Coke. Her friend said, "Shouldn't you get a Diet Coke?"

This question, simple to some, but loaded with implications, caused this young woman to feel as if she were fat, and *should be* on a diet. For many, this question would not have affected them in the least. Its implication would have been immediately dismissed, or met with a tough comeback in order to defend. For others, as this young woman, it hit a deeper wound that can't always be understood at a young age. And it remained the memory that caused the effect of years of yo-yo dieting, shame, guilt, and insecurity.

FEELING YOUR FEELINGS

Take a moment, close your eyes, and think of a similar memory. When ready, write out what emotions you are feeling in this very moment.

What is the strongest emotion?

Is it bringing up anxiety or feelings of sadness, loneliness, or depression?

How has this memory affected your life?

How has this memory affected your relationship with God?

two | it's time to live

"For you were once darkness, but now you are light in the Lord. LIVE as children of light, for light produces goodness, righteousness, and truth."

Ephesians 5:8-9

"No one understands me."

"No one cares about me."

"No one knows what I've been through, or what hardships I've suffered."

"If you only knew what my childhood was like, or the dysfunction of my family."

"My life is stressful and the responsibilities are endless. I can't handle the pressure."

These are reactive responses brought about by the darkness of empty arguments. What lies keep you from living your life fully?

We are not perfect people, which means we are *surrounded* by imperfect people. This creates a great amount of dysfunction, self-centeredness, hardship, suffering, stress, and pressure. Whether

Reclaimed

or not you have suffered mental, verbal, emotional, physical, or sexual abuse, you may feel as if you've skirted by a psychologically healthy life.

It could be your "empty arguments" were the pressures you put upon yourself. Take the list of empty arguments, and learn to move from your state of fear to recognize the gifts and talents God gave you to succeed in living your life more fully.

In both my personal experience, as well working with others who have suffered various emotional and physical abuses, I've found when we reside in the darkness, we find an empty comfort in claiming one of the following realities:

"Bad things always happen to me. I'm unlucky."
– "It's all my fault."

- OR -

"Why does God allow bad things to happen to me?"
– "It's all God's fault."

If you read these two statements and felt defensive with the need to say, "That's not me. I don't feel either way," yet you *still* find yourself "stuck" and unable to overcome this rut in your life, then feel blessed. You are shedding the darkness, walking away from the fear and shame that keeps the rest of us from utilizing our gifts and talents. You recognize you are not in control, but might *still* feel the need for more direction. If this is you, then please feel free to move on to the next chapter. *However*, if either statement above tugs at your heart, then let's continue and see how to shed these lies from your life.

"Bad things always happen to me. I'm unlucky." – *"It's all my fault."*

In my life, in the midst of my darkest time, I hopped back and forth between these two statements. Maybe because I had such a strong relationship with God in my early childhood, so I felt more comfortable taking the blame for my pitfalls, rather than sticking it onto God.

In fact, the times I blamed God were when I thought I was more or less "in control" of my life but knew my situation was less than desirable. I'll go more into this when we discuss "It's all God's fault." However, I spent years in shame and unworthiness. I'll never forget the moment I walked away from *the house*. I went voluntarily to *the house* when I was seventeen years old. I also went knowing I had desired *some* attention. I didn't realize the attention I received would be life-scarring.

I walked away from the house having been date raped by *a friend* I'd known since the sixth grade. Even though I struggled, resisted, and said, "NO," I still felt at fault. Months following, I continued to make conscious decisions to be in places I

Reclaimed

shouldn't be, and scenarios I knew were open to danger. When boys took advantage of me, I didn't resist. I *felt used* anyway, so there was no need to "save" myself any longer. But I felt empty and useless, as if no one could ever see me as "good" again. This led to drinking heavily to numb the pain, which led to waking up hungover and physically in pain. "Why me? Why does this always happen to me?" Yet, I was the one driving myself to the party, taking the drink, going for guys who clearly wanted one thing from me: sex.

Hear me out. If you are a survivor of rape, date rape, or any kind of abuse, it is *not your fault*. However, when we allow what has been done to us to leave us in the dark with empty arguments, then we make decisions based on those empty arguments. This is where we need to wake up and see God's light and know we are not alone.

The same goes for those who haven't been physically abused, but find their life situations to be less than pleasing—especially living through the recent pandemic. Maybe there are no extenuating psychological circumstances, which can be an "excuse" to keep the negative in your life. Especially if it seems as if nothing's going your way, or what you'd prefer to have. Maybe you applied for several jobs, but couldn't seem to land one. Or you have a medical illness—even multiple illnesses—that keep you from living the life you expected to live (this scenario is often geared toward blaming God, too). So, let's say you acknowledged you made some bad choices in your life, suffered the consequences (a bad marriage, drug or alcohol issues, financial trouble, etc.), yet you felt as if you tried to do it all the right way, but nothing went *your way*. One negative after another, after another, so you've thrown your hands up in the air and loudly claimed, "Why me? Nothing good ever happens to me. What am I doing wrong?"

You are listening to the lies, and you have allowed these lies to control your emotional responses and reactions. Now, let's get rid of these lies. No matter who it was who told you these lies, or when they said them to you, *you can get rid of them!* Write them out. For instance, in my case, when I was blaming myself, the lies I kept hearing were:

- Nothing good ever happens to me.
- No one really loves me.
- I'm not smart enough to succeed.
- There is always someone prettier, smarter, more confident, and nicer.
- I dug myself into this hole, and there is no way out.
- If people saw the mess I am inside, they would run away.
- I don't measure up, even if I try, I fail.

REFLECTION ON HEALING

Do any of the lies mentioned in this chapter sound familiar?

What do you *"hear"* when you feel down and unmotivated? What specific words come to mind?

What keeps you from moving forward?

It is vitally important to write these lies out, to expose them, and pull them out of the darkness and into the light. There is a *psychological* connection to the *physicality* of writing them down, and *even* reading ALOUD these lies. These lies weren't produced out of thin air. At some point in your life, you encountered an experience or a person who influenced you, and were left behind with these lies in your wake.

After you write out these lies, immediately write another list creating the opposite to the lie. And be sure to read ALOUD the positive words.

For an example, the opposite to my lies:

- Good happens every day. If you wake-up, it is a good day.
- We are all worthy because God loves us.
- Success is relevant to your dreams and motivation.
- Your level of intelligence is irrelevant, if you have the motivation and desire. If a certain amount of book intelligence is needed to

achieve a desire, then your motivation *will lead you* to the qualified intelligence.
- Beauty, intelligence, personality, and self-esteem are relevant to each individual.
- The great truth about being at the bottom is that the *only* way out is up.
- Every saint is a sinner.
- We all have our ugly baggage, so the more we share, the more we relate and can help one another overcome the lies.
- To *whose* standards am I trying to measure up?
- Maybe I'm looking to please the wrong people. God asks one thing of us, which is to "love one another, as I have loved you."

Recently I spoke with Nancy*, a mother of two elementary-school-aged children, who battled these internal lies. By all outward appearances, she seemed to have what most considered a "perfect life." She was beautiful, in good shape, well-dressed, had a respected position in the corporate world, and was in a good marriage.

So what was the problem? Daily, she felt like a fraud. "I go to all lengths to make sure my kids have the best of everything, and *look the part*. But before I get them out the door, it's like World War II in our house. I'm screaming and yelling, tugging on my little girls' hair, trying to fix it 'just right' as they cry because I'm hurting them. My husband didn't do anything to help, but yelled at me because I yelled at them. By the time I drop them off at school and get to work, I'm ready to crawl under my desk and cry. But I *have to* act like I'm fine. I prepare presentations for meetings, but feel as if I'm twelve and about to make my first speech in front of the class. So, I don't feel like I'm as good as everyone else in the room. I keep hearing, *'I'm not a good mom'* in my head. I'm not a good wife and I don't belong in the job I have. I feel like a failure and I don't know why."

What are her lies?

- I'm a fraud.
- I'm not good enough.
- I'm not perfect like everyone else.
- I'm a bad mom.
- I'm not a good wife.
- I'm not as qualified or smart as everyone else at my workplace.
- I'm a failure.

Together, Nancy and I looked at her "lies" list, and I saw her tear up, as she recognized a common denominator—lack of self-worth. After a moment of reflection, she took a deep breath and said, "They are the same lies I heard growing up. I love my parents, but I never felt like I could measure up to their expectations, especially my mother's.

I did everything for her, because I wanted to make her happy. Yet, my mom was never happy, and I always felt like it was my fault, so I tried harder."

She wiped a tear away from her cheek. "It wasn't until I had my first child when my mom confessed how unhappy she was, because she never got to fulfill her dreams. She got married young, then immediately had kids, and felt stuck. I had no idea." Nancy paused, then said, "I'm acting just like my mother."

How many times have we said to ourselves, "*I don't want to be like my parents*"? Then, as we grew up, we found ourselves in similar circumstances as our parents. Once we're with our own families and careers, we see subtle hints of learned behaviors and responses.

"I'm becoming my mother," I'd groan, when I realized I reacted in a certain manner. Don't get me wrong, there are many behaviors our parents gave to us, which were well worth being learned and lived. However, they were human too and had their own empty arguments list, which had shaped their reactions and responses. Once again, the best way to break this generational chain is to recognize the pattern, then write out the lies to set a new course with your own healthy truths.

On another sheet of paper, I had her list the opposite of every lie:

Reclaimed

- I am who God made me to be, and this is all I *can* be.
- I *am* good enough—because it is being me—I'm uniquely made.
- Perfect is impossible. No one is perfect.
- I love and care for my kids. I am a good mom.
- I love my husband. I am a good wife.
- I was hired by my company because I am qualified. I bring to the table my individuality and my best effort.
- I am a success because I love and am loved.

The opposite of Nancy's empty arguments were her truths, which correlated with her facts. She was a wife, mother, and employee who was loved by her family, loved by God, and qualified with gifts and talents. Once Nancy began to focus on her facts and her truths on a daily basis, she began to feel lighter and more confident in what she was called to do on a daily basis as a wife, mother, and employee.

The empty arguments no longer weighed her down or kept her in the dark with negative thoughts. Once she brought them forward by verbalizing and writing them down, she was released from the chains of negativity and pessimism that had kept her tethered to them.

If all you hear are these negative, empty arguments in your head about how you are not good enough, or nothing good ever happens to you, or you aren't worthy of success, take a moment to write them *all* down. As silly or frustrating as they may seem, *write them out*. Then immediately start writing your second *list of truths*, the opposite of the lies. Read these out loud. It is in this *truth* you will surely find the way to *live your life more fully, as God intended it to be for you.* Remember, the Truth will *set you free!*

"Why does God allow bad things to happen?" – "It's all God's fault."

When I was young, I had a healthy relationship with God. I lived through an extreme, traumatic experience, but I knew He was with me the entire time. In the fifth grade, and through middle school, I wrote in journals and addressed them: "Dear God," telling Him about my day, who I had a crush on, and the troubles my family was going through. As I grew older, the troubles in my family increased, so I felt as if God wasn't listening because nothing got any better.

By the time I was thirteen, a layperson in a Christian church I frequented with friends told me I had to *choose* between the Christian denomination of my family or the denomination he represented. He said that I was old enough to make the choice and to stay clear from what he felt was not a "proper" Christian denomination. For a thirteen-year-old, this came across as *God* telling me the faith of my family was not good enough, therefore, *I* wasn't good enough.

Reclaimed

A schism tore between me and my relationship with God. I no longer wrote in my journals, and gave up on prayer. Family troubles ensued and worsened as I found myself in unpleasant social situations. Then, it became quite easy to blame God for what happened in my family, because I felt He didn't listen to my prayers. After the first date rape, for a time, I felt I had severed any hope of rectifying my relationship with God. I felt such total shame and guilt for what had been done to me, and I felt it was too much for God to see me as anything *but impure*, so thus unworthy.

The decisions I made were carelessly based on my low self-esteem and lack of self-worth. I went along with what everyone else was doing or wanted to do with no regard to my safety or health. The consequences of my decisions were one bad outcome after another. For a while, I held so much anger and resentment toward God for not answering my prayers *the way I expected*. I then blamed Him for the disarray in my life.

I moped about unhappy with my life. "Why is God doing this to me?" This brought on a great amount of jealousy and envy toward others. "Why does God give them everything, and me nothing?" This resentment grew deeper when situations took place that were beyond my control. In my early twenties, I was diagnosed with the autoimmune disease rheumatoid arthritis, which threatened my physical well-being. I felt I *did* nothing to contract

this autoimmune disease, but I believed it *a punishment* for all the other bad decisions I'd made in my life.

Thus, my empty argument: "You are not good enough, so now you have to learn to live a life of hardship." I took this "lie" and held it close to me like a dirty, little secret. For the first two years of diagnosis, the lie swept me into a new pit of despair. Instead of looking out into the world at my options of how to live with this disease and possibly overcome it, I retreated and focused on the negative. "I'll be crippled by the time I'm forty, and no one will want to be around me, much less be married to me."

The pain physically tore through my body as my daily reminder feeding my anger and resentment toward God. The pity party grew exponentially. "What's one more bad thing in my life? I don't matter anyway." The vision of God in my mind had solidified as this mighty power above me wreaking havoc and pain for all my sins. Even as I felt the faint stirrings of my spirit crying out to be in His favor; the negativity of my empty argument, with the deep anger, hardened into *pride*.

All around me, my friends grew closer to God, attending Bible studies and joining groups at their respective churches. At this point, I did only an outward "show," occasionally attending any Christian church my friends supported, but inside, pride kept me from receiving what faith had to offer. In

Reclaimed

my mind, I accepted the "bad things" *done to me or against me*, and I could even accept the "bad decisions" I'd made. But how could I claim ownership for a physical, medical hardship? This one was on God. I just couldn't accept any other explanation of suffering through it except that I must have *deserved* the illness.

The emotional weight of this pride, the hardship, brings a spirit down so low, God has no other choice than to meet you at the bottom. Unfortunately, there were many opportunities given to me to receive the love of God, to accept His love during this time, before I'd actually hit my emotional rock bottom.

In the Bible studies, I felt the stirrings of the truth awakening something within my spirit. Still, my pride would stifle the response with, "I'm not going to let myself get hurt again." After joining a couple's study at our church, I felt myself begin to acknowledge the truth of God's love for me. But then, my pride reminded me, "Don't forget the mistakes you've made."

My pride fought hard. Instead of protecting me, it ended up hurting those I loved. One evening, the anger, resentment, and frustration that had been boiling deep within my spirit rose up and exploded into rage. My two-year-old son stood in the crossfire, and looked at me with fear in his eyes. *I did not want to be the type of person who made my son look at me with fear.*

No longer did it matter whose fault it was—mine, God's, someone else's, fate, karma, whatever—it didn't matter. The stirrings of my spirit broke through the window of opportunity and cried out to God, "I don't want to live this life anymore. I don't want to be this person. If you have something you want to do with my life then do it!" Therein relinquishing all control over to God. The empty arguments were just that—empty.

"I waited, waited for the Lord; who bent down and heard me cry, drew me out of the pit of destruction, out of the mud of the swamp, set my feet upon a rock, steadied my steps, and put a new song in my mouth. Many shall look on in awe, and they shall trust in the Lord."

Psalm 40:2-4

In this vulnerable moment, God showed Himself to me. He spoke love to my heart, and for the first time I received it with openness because the fight was gone. I knew then everything would be fine. To trust in Him daily, as daily was all He sought. One day at a time. One Step at a time. *One moment at a time.*

It took many days, many moments in a day. One day at a time of learning to live in the vulnerable state of trusting God with what His will was for my life. And, with each moment of each day, I saw the sun instead of the clouds. I waited patiently for the promise of the rainbow, instead of focusing on the storms. Slowly, I opened more of my heart and received His words of encouragement. All love and truth for myself, instead of turning them away, assuming they were meant for others more justified—more deserving.

There's no way around suffering, it continues to inflict each one of us. However, if you're willing, God brings good from hardship. The courage and strength born from overcoming tragedy, or fighting illness, refines our spirit. In turn, an exponential outpouring of encouragement and inspiration is brought to others who lived through their own suffering.

Inspiration *cannot* be borne from pride. In fact, every inspirational story heard of hardship overcome was borne from one's desire to *live life fully*. *Existing* is not truly living the way God wants us to live. Likewise, withdrawing inward into pity, self-destruction, blame, or pride breeds only loneliness to you and destruction of those closest to you. Worst case scenario—a pathetic, painful death.

When you choose to live fully through God, you produce goodness, righteousness, and truth.

REFLECTION ON HEALING

When the lies that keep us from our dreams and successes are exposed to God's healing light, our purpose comes alive!

Write your truth. Your truth is what is *concrete*, something no one else can argue. What is your job? What have you accomplished at this point? This is about focusing on the positive, which no one else can take away from you. So, always *focus* on the positive. We take power away from the negative when we focus on the positive.

Read what you have written out loud. It is your truth. This might seem ridiculous and you may choose to skip this step, but trust me. It matters. I wrote a bio for my Speaker Sheet, which essentially is exactly what you are doing when writing out your truth. I simply wrote out the facts of my accomplishments. When I read it out loud, it affected me on an emotional level to hear what I had achieved, even through the years I had felt so dark and negative.

Claim it. This is your life! Own it. We are our own worst critic when we should be our greatest fan and supporter. Claiming your truth, the positive in your life, does not make you egocentric. Acknowledging your accomplishments means you are a healthy individual who knows how to appreciate the gifts in others, because you can appreciate the gift in yourself.

Reclaimed

LIVE IT. How you live this life, how you respond to it and move forward, is only on you. No one else will be able to do this for you. It's time to live the life you know you deserve.

three | you are the key

You Are Stronger Than You Realize

"Try to learn what is pleasing to the Lord."

Ephesians 5:10

Get over it!

What do those words do to you when you hear them from someone you love—your significant other, family members, close friends, acquaintances, or even coworkers? Do you get angry? Frustrated? Cringe with guilt? Feel ashamed because apparently whatever it was you were going through should be *easy to "fix"*?

Are you tired of others trying to "fix" you? Men and women can *both* feel this way, but men, let's be honest. . .it's in the male gene to want to "fix" things. I've come across many women who find themselves flustered, frustrated, and in many ways disregarded because they weren't looking for an answer when they shared something, but rather *to be heard, to be listened to*.

Reclaimed

The next directive Paul gave through Ephesians 5:10 was: *"Try to learn what is pleasing to the Lord."* The first word given is *"try."*

Yes, *try*. Paul didn't begin with the command "learn." Paul knew the internal struggles of those he ministered. He had to overcome a great amount of internal and external persecution and hardship when he wrote this letter to the people of Ephesus. He addressed them with care and concern, acknowledging their struggles with empty arguments, which created their various spiritual and emotional wounds.

When my boys were little and received a task before them that seemed daunting and unmanageable, they came up with a thousand excuses as to why they couldn't complete the task. Excuse after excuse was given, even before they tried. "How do you know you *can't* do it if you don't try?" I'd ask. With my support and encouragement, they mustered up whatever courage they needed to try. And, I admit, many times they failed.

But immediately when they failed, I'd back them up to have them try again. "Try, try, try again," I'd quip, so often, they'd say it before I could get the full sentence completed.

"I can't," I'd hear occasionally, with defeat and devastation in their voice. *"Can't never could,"* I'd retort and though I might have received a few "eye rolls" for that one, they'd try again. Eventually, the task did get completed. The smiles, puffed-up chests of pride, and confidence from overcoming the fear of "trying" then accomplishing the task became an affirmation to never give up.

Never give up.

One of my favorite quotes by Winston Churchill is on a magnet on my fridge:

"Never, never, never give up."

Even after my twenty-two-year marriage ended in divorce, I still looked at the magnet and knew I did not give up. My ex-husband may disagree as I made the final decision to dissolve the marriage. It may have *seemed* like I "gave up.' But to those who were my closest confidants, spiritual advisors, and therapists who counseled me through the various trials and tribulations knew. They each helped me to decipher the false and empty arguments in order to feel worthy enough to embrace my truth. . .they knew I *tried*. What I did *not* give up on was myself. Not an advocate for divorce, rather, I do believe in the covenant of marriage. It takes a true type of commitment and an exuberant amount of work, which was why I stayed married for over two decades! However, I would be remiss to not acknowledge that certain circumstances by themselves can muddy up the clear waters of any relationship. When you mix in the gravel and dirt carried over from unhealed past abuses, then the water can turn into cement.

I spent the first half of my life figuring out how to make everyone else happy. This meant I worked diligently at "fixing" whatever, at the time, but left my shell broken. No matter how hard I tried, nothing could take away the emptiness and loneliness inside me. The molestation abuse incurred by my grandfather, from three to six years old, took away my healthy boundaries. We all were supposed to learn as children to be able to speak up when something wasn't right, or didn't feel good. Because of the abuse, and being told *not to speak* of it, I spent years in therapy trying to find my voice, to feel okay for *not* being in agreement with someone. I had to figure out what I desired because I was groomed to put everyone else's wants, desires, and needs before my own. I know I am not alone, growing up in a family where alcohol and drug addiction kept me on my toes. It also laid the groundwork to become extremely codependent, and simply piled onto the empty arguments, it didn't take long to lose myself completely.

    Not until I attended a recovery meeting for family members who have addiction in their family did I hear the idiom "first things first." In this same meeting, I came to receive the truth—*"You can't change anyone, but yourself."* All those years, I fruitlessly spent trying to be what I thought was needed in order to make those around me happy! Thus, I never even knew what happiness meant to me as an individual. So, I then had to try and find my joy. *First things first*; I worked at it one layer at a time.

Whatever it is you are feeling that has you desperate to find joy, hope, and happiness, you can, and will, get through this, as long as you *try* and *never give up*. You do *deserve* this healing, so please *try*.

Now, if you are willing to try the key, "learn what is *pleasing* to the Lord." A very simple directive, yet often made complicated.

What pleases the Lord?

"The sacrifice of the wicked is an abomination to the LORD, but the prayer of the upright is his delight."

Proverbs 15:8

Prayer pleases the Lord. I used to struggle with prayer, when in the midst of my deepest battle, because I wasn't sure if I knew *how* to pray. Prayer is simply being in a conversation with God, so in reality, there's no right or wrong way to pray. He's delighted in knowing your desire to come to Him.

One of the simplest forms of prayer I've often used is to follow ACTS:

A – Adoration: Tell God hello, say good morning, or good evening, or simply, "Hi." If you feel comfortable in your relationship with God, acknowledge who He is to you. For example, "Good morning, Lord, you are so gracious and merciful." If you don't feel comfortable with this form of adoration *try* a simple "Hi God."

C - Confession: Talk to God about what is on your mind. Confess to Him about your rage, anger, frustration, or sadness. *Even if it is toward Him.* God can handle it. The cool thing is, God already knows what is on your heart, but the healing process begins when *you* choose to talk it out *with Him*.

T - Thanksgiving: When you have spent all your energy pouring out the empty arguments, the nasty thoughts, and even the shameful behaviors or reactions, then take time to talk to God about what makes you most thankful or grateful. Everyone, no matter how dire their situation, can find *at least three things* in their lives to be thankful *for*, such as another day of life, your children, your spouse, your pets, glorious nature, it did or didn't rain, or you found a penny on the ground. *Anything.* When we take the time to *focus on the positive*, it reminds us there is something more to see than the situation before us.

S - Supplication (Intercession): This is the time to ask God *specifically* for the needs of others and even ourselves. Be specific. For instance, if your mother is going to the doctor for a routine checkup, then ask God to bless the checkup, and for a positive result.

If heading into a difficult situation at work and you feel ahead of time it may cause you anxiety, then ask God to ease your mind and spirit. For any reason, ask Him to calm your nerves, to take away any fear that causes anxiety, to help you feel more comfortable and sure of what you are to do. If a friend is suffering a marriage crisis, ask God to bless both parties so they can come to a place of love and understanding. God does not limit what or how many blessings you ask for. "Ask and you shall receive." And close with: "In Jesus Christ I pray, Amen!"

"Then let us no longer judge one another, but rather resolve never to put a stumbling block or hindrance in the way of a brother. I know and am convinced in the Lord Jesus that nothing is unclean in itself; still, it is unclean for someone who thinks it unclean. If your brother is being hurt by what you eat, your conduct is no longer in accord with love. Do not because of your food destroy him for whom Christ died. So do not let your good be reviled. For the kingdom of God is not a matter of food and drink, but of righteousness, peace, and joy in the Holy Spirit; whoever serves Christ in this way is pleasing to God and approved by others."

Romans 14:13-18

When you find yourself praying daily, begin and end your day in His presence. Give your day over to Him, be thankful, and take time to pray specifically for your needs and others. Then, your spirit naturally *desires* to treat those around you the way He would want you to treat them. By not judging, flaunting others' weaknesses in front of them, or devaluing their time. Seek peace, righteousness, and joy as you encourage others to follow by your own actions.

"But without faith it is impossible to please Him, for anyone who approaches God must believe that He exists and that He rewards those who seek Him."

Hebrews 11:6

I grew up going to church. Not just the Catholic church, but many other Christian denominations. However, growing up, I learned more about each denomination than I did about embracing the faith. When I suffered through some of my most difficult struggles during my teenage years, I left God behind. I chose my first step because I believed I had failed Him. At the time, I felt as if I could not live up to any standard God had for me because of all the bad decisions I'd made resulting from what had been done to me. I never knew God loved me *no matter what I'd done*.

Church was more about tradition. What you had to, or were supposed to do. What you couldn't do, to be *accepted* and loved. And, what your family made you do. I had witnessed what faith was through my grandmother. She was a devout Catholic, prayed four rosaries a day, sat on the front row pew in Mass, every morning, as well every Sunday. Her little brown prayer book was weathered, brittle, and falling apart, held together by a stretched rubber band. She exemplified the tradition, but she also *lived out the faith*. There was no doubt in my mind that she *believed* in God, in His promises and His love for her.

Even though she felt comfort in the rote prayers of the rosary or in her prayer book, faith poured out of her lips, not just saying the prayers, but offering them to God. Faith was in her heart. She'd grasp my hand during the Lord's Prayer, and I'd feel her squeeze during "*as we forgive those who trespassed against us.*"

I witnessed faith through Sweetgraw, my dad's mother. Actually, I learned about patience and faith from both of my dad's parents, which helped me to keep trust with my elders despite what my other grandfather had done. But I never came to desire faith until I was desperate for something more than the empty arguments that had ruled my life. So I began to pray. I gave it a *try*. Then, on one fateful night when I ended up on the floor, face down, beyond desperate but done, I knew all I wanted was to "*please the Lord.*"

He *saved* me. Not, "accept Jesus Christ, as your personal Lord and Savior, so you are saved" type of saved, but rather he *saved me from me*. I truly was my worst enemy—the thoughts in my head, the personal put-downs, lack of self-respect, and the selfishness. They had led me to more self-destruction than any harm an outsider could have inflicted. He showed Himself to me the evening I poured my heart and soul out to Him. I *sought* Him out and He *saved* me.

"First of all, then, I ask that supplications, prayers, petitions, and thanksgivings be offered for everyone, for kings and for all in authority, that we may lead a quiet and tranquil life in all devotion and dignity. This is good and pleasing to God our savior."

1 Timothy 2:1-3

Finally, understand that in conversation with God, what pleases Him is to look beyond your own personal situations and pray for others. Specifically, He wants to hear us ask for a "quiet and tranquil life," which can be received through devotion to God. I know this might be a bit troublesome for those who were in situations that led them to feel they had to "please," or could never *please* someone in authority. This phrase "to please" may even make you uncomfortable, or be a full-on trigger, depending on what you might have experienced in the past. God wants what is best for you, and He has it prepared for you to receive, but you have to be willing to receive, as well as *know* you are *worth* receiving it. With this knowl-

edge, and understanding of what God longs for us, is where *our intention* of wanting to "please" should originate. And what pleases Him most is when we look beyond ourselves and pray for the needs of others. It truly makes God happy when *you are pleased*.

Sounds perfect, right? Don't we all strive for tranquility? Especially in these moments of your life, living through whatever struggle had you in a bind, a tranquil moment probably sounds divine. We've learned we can strive to acquire moments in a tranquil life simply through prayer, but what is dignity?

Dignity is believing in yourself, having self-respect, and *behaving* this way. In other words, *loving yourself unconditionally*—faults, mistakes, frailties and all—the way God loves us. We are *sometimes* our greatest struggle, our worst critic, and at times, enemy. We won't *accept* we deserve to be loved, to be liked, or even to be forgiven. Because we hold onto this most destructive empty argument, it keeps us separated from God, therefore keeping us from living a happy life which is pleasing to Him.

What keeps us *from wanting* to please the Lord, or being able to please the Lord?

"And those who are in the flesh cannot please God."

Romans 8:8

When I'd venture into inquiring about my faith and contemplate attending a Bible study, I'd think, "*I don't want to be a 'Jesus freak.'"* The desire was there to learn more, but there was an empty argument that stood between me and the desire to "want to please the Lord." When I was in high school, I associated Christians as hypocrites. Being a Christian and a hypocrite went hand-in-hand because I felt looked down upon and judged by the boys and girls who toted *a cloak* of Christianity. Now that I am an adult and can look back with growth and maturity, I acknowledge they weren't hypocrites, rather, I was jealous of the relationship I knew they had with God, and one another.

In reality, I was subconsciously unhappy with my own behavior. Then I projected my unhappiness onto their perceived judgments of me and others, as they refrained from those behaviors we had enlisted or bought into. To me, a *Jesus freak* was someone who proclaimed WWJD (What Would Jesus Do) proudly. They used it against us when they judged our behaviors or actions to be offensive or simply wrong. In hindsight, this was my own judgment of a group who didn't know me, nor I them.

Another empty argument that kept me from seeking a close relationship with God was the fear I would lose my personality. Despite the negativity and anger I harbored inside, I did enjoy my quick wit and sassiness. Living a life that was "pleasing to the Lord" appeared to be boring and dull. Again, assumptions and personal judgments of how a

Christian lived and dressed brought to mind laced-collared blouses, ankle skirts, and the loss of my personality. It was interesting to admit, though, that I believed in Jesus Christ, as well the saving grace of His crucifixion with the resurrection. I just never *felt worthy* of embracing the title of a "Christian." If I couldn't *live* it, how could I *claim* it?

I knew *living in the flesh* was seeking approval through the material world and what I felt it had to offer. Yet, so desperate to be *as good as* those who had *received* more—more money, larger houses, fit and trim bodies, better looks, and so forth—it haunted me. No matter how close it got to me, it never seemed to *satisfy*. My deep, black hole inside of lack and rejection could never be filled.

What does pleasing the Lord have to do with what I'm feeling now or letting go?

"Similarly, an athlete cannot receive the winner's crown, except by competing according to the rules."

2 Timothy 2:5

Our spirits will never be satisfied, until we align our will with God's will for our life.

"My days were shaped, before one came to be."

Psalm 139:16

So, God has written out our days. He knows the best journey for us to travel in order to achieve our purposes. When we take detours because of our lack of trust, faith, or out of sheer resistance, our spirits will remain unsatisfied. So, if you are in a state of unrest, anxiety, worry, melancholy, or general unhappiness about your life, those are the *warning* signs. You've detoured and gotten lost or are headed in the wrong direction.

My moment of letting go was like a collision of wills—mine versus His. He allowed me to see how the effect of *pleasing the flesh* extended beyond my journey, but harmed the ones I loved. When I could finally look beyond myself, I knew all I had left was to accept what God had in mind for me. This meant letting go and *trying* to please Him.

REFLECTION ON HEALING

One year on a retreat, I watched a short video depicting God's love for us. The storyline was a little boy had done something his parents told him not to, and he knew he had done wrong. He felt an immense amount of shame and guilt, so he hid under the covers in his parents' bed to avoid facing his father. The father lovingly pulled him out from under the covers and held him tight. "Nothing you could ever say or do would ever make me love you

less," was the message from the loving father to his child.

This is the same message for us. We are not perfect. And if something has been done or said to us that caused shame and guilt, it is not our shame or guilt *to own*. When we make our own decisions that lead into sin, we are met by a loving, forgiving Father who wants to make sure we know his only concern is that we don't harm ourselves or others. That is what sin really is. Harming ourselves and others. *Nothing* we can ever say or do will ever make our Father love us less.

When did you feel your closest connection with God? Or have you ever felt a close connection with God?

Do you feel disconnected from God? What does this disconnection feel like? Is it emptiness? Loneliness? Unworthiness?

Do you feel judged by God?

Can you feel God's love now?

Reclaimed

Scar Tissue

Trauma does not have to be physical,
as the emotional has many unseen scars.
The pain runs deeper than broken bones.

Some words lose their meaning -
like - 'I love you' - when bantered
around, or reiterated, or corrupted,
when used to cover-up abuse.

Past wounds may heal with time,
or a change of words when
a new romance blossoms.

Yet, if completely naive and lost,
one needs to practice discernment
amidst chaos. So know, only real
love is more powerful than fear.

Throughout this time-struggle,
a profound sense of aloneness,
of disconnection from everyone.

Then, I allowed the Light to come to me,
my empty heart and soul opened-up.
I started to find peace with my life,
glimmers of true beauty of its existence.

Shannon M. McGraw

Those first steps to new avenues - pathways,
transmuted into something stronger and brighter.
I felt the compassion, love and tenderness.

Looking back, God's alchemy for me,
to feel wiser, more balanced. And, accepting
the new joy in my heart and soul,
to breathe, expand, melting into Love.

Alice Parker © 2020

*four | illuminate
the darkness*

"Take no part in the fruitless works of darkness; rather expose them."

Ephesians 5:11

Imagine the heaviness you feel inside at this moment, literally, a jumbled-up mix of words and events disguised as maggots crammed into the darkest recesses of your inner spirit. They are like parasites feeding off of your security, worth, and emotional state. As long as they remain hidden and untouched, they multiply exponentially. It's not until you are forced to expose them out of sheer insanity, as they get the best of you, inhabiting every aspect of your being—your mind, body, *and spirit*.

I envision the movie with Tom Hanks called *Green Mile*. The main character, John Coffey, a gigantic man, has a special ability to *"suck-out the ugly"* from someone and release it to the light.

The way the movie depicted the "ugly" is that it came out like a multitude of minuscule moths that poured out from John's mouth. Usually, the person he helped was irritable and negative, as well often suffering some physical ailment. After Coffey sucked the "ugly" out of the person, they would be free from the ailment, with a lighter spirit, and a more generous and joyful disposition. John would then look up to the sky, open his mouth, and exhale the "ugly" until every last bit was out of his system.

Unfortunately, there is no John Coffey to come do the work for us and suck out our ugly. But I do believe the overall result can be the same. When we sort out what all lies within our deepest, darkest recesses, we can then expose them to the light. We are not only benefitting our spirit to be cleansed, but often our physical health is also improved.

Ugly goes beyond empty arguments. *Ugly is the actual actions or words spoken* to us that have remained within us, multiplying to eat us up. Every "ugly" may be different to each individual. And sometimes, we have so much "ugly" it's hard to get beyond the obvious attacks to find the remaining offenses that linger, buried so deeply.

Ugly can be abuse—mental, physical, sexual, emotional, verbal, or even spiritual.

Ugly can be fears brought on by past or ongoing events.

Ugly can be feeling second-best, being cheated on by a significant other, passed over for a promotion, or a consistent struggle with weight, or other personal situations holding you back from feeling good about yourself.

Ugly can be seriously affecting your health, like having an eating disorder, or struggling with self-mutilation, even drugs, or alcohol.

Ugly is anything and everything that makes you feel fruitless in being able to change it. By keeping it within you, it harbors nothing of value. Instead, it continually attacks your spirit and slowly erodes your feelings of worth to eventually snuff out your light.

REFLECTION ON HEALING

What makes up your "ugly"? It can be one major thing, or a multitude of little, petty references accumulating into a bigger ugly at your core. Whatever it is, *expose* it right now. Expose it to the light of God, and *it is* dissolved away.

Because I believe in teaching by example, I will give you an example of writing out my "ugly" at the point of writing this book, because a part of me felt I deserved it: incest, date rape, emotional abuse throughout various stages of my life to this point, insecurity about so many things, infidelity, betrayal, fear of success, and cancer.

Our "ugly" can be something done to us that was not in our realm of control, and an "ugly" can be because of our own decisions or choices. In no way am I responsible for having been raped by my grandfather, nor raped by the young men when I was younger. Because it was done to me then left scars of shame and guilt. I realize it is a major aspect of my "ugly," the lies that dictated so much of my reactions and responses. However, I also won't allow it to be my excuse for the rest of my "ugly." I am the one who made decisions to have relationships that shouldn't have been, or to avoid opportunities because I convinced myself I wasn't good enough. In my same breath, a big part of my "ugly" is because of what was done by others in my relationships, which ultimately caused me to feel less than or not enough.

Reclaimed

Cancer? Well, sickness is ugly. We don't cause it. We don't seek it. And rarely can we determine which way it will go. I wrote my experience of having gone through thyroid cancer as an ugly because the radiation left me feeling bloated, unattractive, and quite literally poisoned. However, in the same breath, I could say cancer is my *truth*. It happened. It remains a part of my life because I've managed to find the positive in the journey, so I can embrace it.

Write *all* your "ugly" down. Right Now. No need for details or description. One word or phrase is all you need to share.

Keep this page in your journal or notebook marked, because this might be a good reference to come back to if you feel the need to discuss your empty arguments and "ugly" to a therapist.

Success! By writing it down, you have already taken a huge step in exposing it to the light. Now, Jesus can work on it with you, because you are *willing* to let Him.

Sometimes, a little of the "ugly" holds tight and remains within us, only peeking out its ugly head when triggered. A sight, sound, smell, word, gesture, even taste can be all it needs to crawl out of the deepest, darkest recesses of its cave.

When this happens, it's important to acknowledge it for what it is. For instance, because I'm an incest survivor, certain smells or odd touches can cause a blindsiding reaction. Before I was able to expose this "ugly," the truth of being molested by my grandfather, I never understood *why* or *where* this was coming from. I'd let those terrible feelings totally take over my body and emotions. Something as simple as being in my spin class prompted a weird reaction to set me off into a foul mood for the rest of the day. When this kept happening, I eventually gave up spin class even though it had been one of my most favorite activities to stay in shape.

But, once I began to expose my ugly and pay attention to these sudden responses to feelings, senses, smells, and touch, I recognized I was being "triggered." I went back to my spin class, so when it happened, I acknowledged it by saying to myself, "I know why I'm feeling this way, and *now know I have nothing to fear.*" It's not easy because triggers can be powerful and can affect your spirit deeply. But I put my mind on the song, or the pain in my legs, or I ride faster. If I know there is something else that I can do to make the trigger go away so it keeps me on the bike or whatever, then I do it. For me, it's about *not allowing* my "ugly" to win.

I'm in control because God is in control of me. I can choose to allow the trigger to prevent me from moving forward, or I can choose to find ways to acknowledge it for what it is. I learned to "*catch*" myself, to train my mind to direct it differently. No, this isn't easy. And, it takes persistent practice. I know and I acknowledge it. But it *is* doable. It takes a *retraining* of the mind and, to be honest, putting up the fight where the fight is needed—against the ugly.

Reclaimed

YOU ARE WORTH THE EFFORT

Are you open enough to receive this truth? You are worthy. You are good enough. You *are* enough. You are not meant to hold the guilt and shame any "ugly" often breeds. All of those nasty maggot-like things, I explained at the beginning, they are foreign objects that do not belong anywhere in you or around you.

And if your "ugly" is something you have done, harm you have caused, or if the ugly caused you to add more ugly to the infestation... own up to your mistakes, own up to your own actions, *seek forgiveness*, because you are worthy of forgiveness. But do not take on the guilt or shame of the actions of someone else, which was put upon you. That is for their own journey of redemption, to shed their ugly of the guilt and shame from the actions they put upon you.

I'm in my forties and it took me four decades to fully receive the truth that I was worthy of this forgiveness. I didn't *need to own* the shame or guilt brought onto me by the abuse of my grandfather or the rapists. There were definite mistakes I made that heaped more than enough ugly upon the ugly brought on by others. And I eventually came to understand how to separate the two. I repented for my own actions, sought forgiveness for them, and changed my behaviors. Thus, in doing my part, I came to find an easier *path to forgiving* my grandfather, my rapists, and anyone else who had harmed me emotionally or betrayed me. The more I was active in scooping out the infestation of the ugly from the darkness and exposing it to the light of God's truth, the easier it was to recognize the triggers. Stopping them gave me the energy to redirect them, or even dissolve them completely.

It's a process, as said at the beginning—a Step-Process. Be kind to yourself. Keep *trying*.

REFLECTION ON HEALING

Our "ugly" doesn't represent who we are or who we were created to be. When you look back at the page of the "ugly," it is merely a page of lies and it doesn't represent *who* you are on the inside.

What feelings or reactions do you have when you see in front of you the words and phrases you have chosen to represent your "ugly"?

When you look back at the ugly, or phrases and words represented, which have kept you down in the dark? Are you able to turn the page with confidence to a new chapter of life? Never forget, in the light of your truth, who you were created to be—wonderfully made.

"I praise you because I am fearfully and wonderfully made; your works are wonderful, I know that full well."

Psalm 139:14

If your struggle is accepting the reality you can and will overcome all that has kept you in the dark, read the Bible verse above every night before going to bed. You were not made to keep the poison of the past inside. You are wonderfully made and meant to shine bright!

five | awake my soul

"Everything exposed by the light becomes visible, for everything visible becomes light. Therefore, it says: 'Awake, O sleeper, and arise from the dead and Christ will give you light.'"

Ephesians 5:13-14

Now, you've exposed your "ugly" and written down your "empty arguments," so it's time to stop the blame-game. When you surrender control over to God, you are then *in control* for the first time because you are following *His will*.

Your surrender gives you freedom or free will to choose! You realize you are in control of where your mind goes, what thoughts will invade your space, and how you'll respond better instead of reacting negatively. Amazing.

However, with this freedom or control of choice comes *a lot of responsibility*. We have to own up to our decisions and recognize we *made* them. No longer can we say, "I hurt you because you hurt me!"

Reclaimed

or worse, "I hurt you because someone hurt me ten years ago!" No more blaming our past on our present. Your past *does not* define who you are. It may have sculpted you in various ways, giving smooth lines in some areas and cracks or crevices in others. But, and this is very important, *your past does not represent the entire masterpiece.*

I've worked with many people who have suffered unimaginable travesties. And, with every single person who has overcome, they have learned the vital steps in life of "letting go." They thank God for every single, tainted, nasty, ugly moment, because it has fortified their character. They have become empowered by such gifts as patience, vulnerability, perseverance, tenacity, compassion, empathy, and strength. *You also* have these gifts, but you need to allow yourself the opportunity to discover them within you.

Recently, I was called to direct a women's retreat for my home parish, and one of the women on my team was in need of assistance. She and her daughter had been in a wreck, which totaled her car, so she needed a ride to pick up her prescriptions. I assumed she was picking up prescriptions for injuries sustained from the wreck. I was wrong. Linda* *already* had a bag full of prescription bottles with her when she climbed into my vehicle.

Curiosity rarely keeps me from minding my own business. "What is in the bag?"

"They are medications I have to take from my heart and breast surgery," she said more matter of fact than I would've managed, if it were me.

"Seriously?" I couldn't hide my shock. "What kind of heart and breast surgery?"

"I had a heart transplant a little over two years ago, and a few months ago they discovered inflammatory breast cancer. They had to remove two segments of my right breast. I couldn't do chemotherapy, though, because of the heart transplant." She looked at me, as if she'd undergone something as simple as a wart removed.

Later, sitting in the waiting area of the pharmacy while they cleared up some insurance issues with her prescriptions, she told me more about the health issues she'd encountered throughout her life. The heart problems, since childhood, had led to the heart transplant, kidney failure, and the breast cancer. Then, when she was in her early twenties, she discovered she was pregnant, though she'd been told she couldn't conceive. The doctors wanted her to abort the baby, but she refused, even though she'd been told her heart was too weak.

Through prayer, and her determined perseverance, she continued to pray throughout her pregnancy, asking both she and her daughter would be healthy. When her prayers were answered, she knew she could trust in His plan for her life. "He al-

Reclaimed

lowed me to have my daughter, but He didn't heal me completely. . .it's okay. Don't get me wrong, there are moments I cry in the shower because it's too much. Or sometimes I get angry because I don't think I can handle anything more. But then I remember my daughter and all God *has* done for me, and I feel His peace." Again, her honesty and being so forthright amazed me.

Living on disability, and now without a car, Linda could have spent the evening checking off her misfortunes, one fact after another; instead she gave me her story in short. She then chose to talk about her daughter's great accomplishments. Her daughter, a junior in high school, was already pursued by the best of the best universities, which were willing to give full scholarships for her to attend. She wanted to go to medical school, to become a pediatrician. Like her mother, she's also faithful beyond measure, often choosing church activities or service projects over a regular teen's social life.

Linda does not allow her illnesses to define her days. She meets them head on and does whatever's necessary to survive for her daughter. She never falls into being a victim of her illnesses. She often speaks at our downtown medical center to other patients who are going through similar procedures. She's a woman who lives by hope, and she offers hope by being a living example. Mainly, Linda's ability to be confident and secure, even in the face of her multiple trials, comes because she *believes* in who she is within God. She *believes* in His love for her. And, she totally *believes* in His promises.

Popular speaker and author Beth Moore wrote a short segment in her book titled, *Believing God*,[1] where she described how she lived for years with a belief system of knowing God's love. She'd heard the messages through His word and wanted to believe she was "*this*." A "this" was whatever positive she sought at the time. A good person. A good mom. A good friend, and so on. But instead, she lived out her life unable to accept it, arguing, "No, Lord, I am *that*,"—one of the hurtful things she thought about herself. She went on to write, "Months turned into years, and the voice of God grew increasingly insistent: 'Beth, when will you ever believe you are *this*?' He was getting me to the point where even though I may have felt like a *that*, he wanted me to be thinking like a *this*."

For a long time, Beth Moore essentially "faked it till she felt it." She finally went against the empty arguments in her mind and insisted she was a *this*, even though she was used to hearing and feeling like a *that*. I read this short passage and it hit home to me.

> All of my life, I had this empty argument plague every aspect of my life, as it told me

---

[1] Moore, Beth   "Believing God" B&H Publishing Group 2008

"*You are not good enough.*" Even if I managed to achieve a goal, or accomplishment or find success, I still felt *not good enough*. For years, I had to "fake it till I made it." God had given me the directive of Ephesians. I was doing my best to weed-out the empty arguments, and live the life He had planned for me. Opportunity after opportunity came, as I was given the chance to speak and tell my story in front of others. I felt confident in what God had done in my life, and I even knew this was His path for me. Yet, after every speaking engagement, regardless of the accolades and praise, what I heard in my head was, "*It wasn't good enough.*"

I never understood why I allowed one stray, empty argument to get the best of me. Quickly, the little lie affected my confidence and the ability I'd originally received as a blessing from God. When I began to question these abilities, I knew this one lie was a slow fade back into the darkness. I didn't want to sink into the pit again. So, I prayed. I cried out to God, "*Why do I not feel good enough? What keeps me from feeling the confidence I know I can have, but can't seem to reach?*" The interesting aspect of this prayer was that I could actually feel within me a truth scratching its way to the surface. I knew subconsciously that I'd been shoving it back down, unwilling to accept it for fact. As I cried out in desperation for answers, I could feel my spirit's internal struggle to see my ugly—all of it.

God is gracious in His timing, and He knew when I could receive it, when I was able to accept my ugly in order to fully heal, I would. Then, one fateful day, as I wrote in *Redeemed*, something triggered a memory from when I was a very young girl. Sights, sounds, and smells rushed forth, along with the memories. I knew fully the source of the empty argument had finally scratched its way through. As previously said, I was molested by my grandfather. I'd known he'd molested my mother, and also molested my sister. *But* I just hadn't been able to consider myself to have been a victim as well. However, once these memories surfaced and I accepted them as truly real, I found myself doubled over on the floor. I wailed uncontrollably from the pain of the secret, which had been deeply buried for so long. Amazingly, as it tore through me, I simultaneously felt peace and wholeness.

It made sense. My life made sense. And now, I knew why I heard this empty argument, because I'd been deceived. I'd been told in countless ways, not just verbally, but by this sick behavior of his, *I was not good enough*. As a little girl, deep inside, his action had made me not feel good enough to be *whole*, good enough to ever feel *secure*, and especially not good enough to be *normal*. I recognized the ugly, the unadulterated lie, for what it was. So, I no longer faked the belief of I am *"this"*—God's beloved daughter, *more than* good enough to be a vessel for Him to work through. And, good enough to receive His redemptive grace. Those lies, those empty arguments, were just that—empty. Don't allow any excuses to become more empty arguments. You deserve more!

REFLECTION ON HEALING

Out of all the empty arguments and "ugly" you've been able to write down, which one plagues you the most? Many of us have one constant nag, buried deep in the back of our everyday subconscious.

On my computer screen, I have as my screen saver the message YOU ARE ENOUGH. There are many days it comes across my screen at the very moment I need to be reminded of who I am, who I *really* am, and to discard the lie that wants to creep back in.

Locate yours and write it out!

My friend, *you* are enough.

You are worthy.

You are capable.

You are strong.

You are courageous.

You are more than your past mistakes.

You are loved *unconditionally by God and hopefully by yourself!*

Reclaimed

Sonnet - "The Lady"
By Daniel Martin

ABAB, CDCD, EFEF, GG

The light was blackened
but a love drew me nearer
I see my hope now awakened
As the shadows disappear
I thought I was lost
you became the only way
When the waves of life tossed
I thought I was too far astray

My hope is now bound
There is no more price to pay
Your life in me is found
you are here to stay

Heaven is as lovely as a new smile
I'll hold you in my heart forever in a while

six | claim your inner wisdom

"Watch carefully then how you live, not as foolish persons but as wise, making the most of the opportunity, because the days are evil."

Ephesians 5:15-16

The enemy's grip is like a vice. It shackles even the strongest of wills. When we've been in captivity for so long, we forget how we got there, so immediately take on the responsibility for not being able to get away.

"I can't speak about what's been done to me because no one will believe me. I should have walked away. I could have told someone. I should not have made the decision to go there, do that, or say what I said." Don't get caught up in the *could haves or should haves*. The past is not yours to take back. What is in your godly control is focusing on your moments today and not allowing the past to de-

termine your decisions. Nor allow the future to paralyze you from where God wants to move within you today.

God doesn't look at just your *potential*. When God looks at you, He sees who He *knows* you are, what you can do and what you will do, once *you decide* to be on His team. Remember, Jesus never healed anyone who didn't first *admit to being sick*. And there is a difference in admitting and taking on the blame. The enemy is clever, and before we realize it, we've either taken on the responsibility of the suffering, or put it on someone else.

I've been speaking with a survivor, I'll call her Anne, for the past seven years. The introduction of our mentor/survivor relationship began in the most unlikely venues: Twitter. I'd just founded Hopeful Hearts Ministry and was learning how to tweet inspirational messages. Anne replied to one of my messages asking me, "How?" How could she heal?

After a few Skype and phone conversations, I found out she'd been abused by a family member her entire childhood. I was the only one she had ever told. She wouldn't even tell her therapist. She hadn't told her husband, and of course, she'd never tell her family. The fact she went to therapy was a consolation, as I realized what she'd been through had been very dark and deeply seated. When I'd broach the subject of her revealing the truth to her therapist, she'd follow it up with a litany of excuses regarding why the therapist wouldn't believe her.

"I should've told someone. I should've run away. I probably asked for it, I was a hellion." And on, and on, her ownership of the guilt and shame continued.

Truthfully, there was nothing more I could do for her, except to listen when she needed to talk, and pray for her. Otherwise, she'd chosen to remain a victim since she'd not taken advantage of the help that was virtually at her fingertips. After a while, our conversations were less frequent, so I assumed she was either hopefully getting the help she needed, or she had fallen far back into the victim personality. I'd hoped to hear from her again once she found the courage to speak up. This might sound troubling to some, but it's a clear example of "needing to take ownership in our healing." *No one* can make the ugly go away for you. It takes work, and often the work is very painful. But, if we keep trying, when we come out the other side of it, we become totally empowered, emerging with a new, vibrant, healthy, strong skin. A real, true transformation like no other, knowing God is on your side, guiding your life into living it fully.

In my marriage, I struggled with intimacy and felt like a failure. I didn't want to admit to failure, so I never admitted how I struggled. This internal battle was what I once considered my "thorn" in my side. In reality, I didn't know how to talk about it, and got little support.

Reclaimed

> *"Therefore, in order to keep me from becoming conceited, I was given a thorn in my flesh, a messenger of Satan, to torment me. [8] Three times I pleaded with the Lord to take it away from me. [9] But he said to me, 'My grace is sufficient for you, for my power is made perfect in weakness.' Therefore, I will boast all the more gladly about my weaknesses, so that Christ's power may rest on me. [10] That is why, for Christ's sake, I delight in weaknesses, in insults, in hardships, in persecutions, in difficulties. For when I am weak, then I am strong."*
>
> *2 Corinthians 12:7-10*

I desired intimacy, both sexual and emotional. Yet, when I got face-to-face, body-to-body, situation-to-situation, I froze. For this, I didn't have distinctive triggers to work through, to make it better. Rather, I had an emotional overload of empty arguments, which I'd allowed to wreak havoc and take control. Five years into the marriage, I cried and tried, even forced it. By ten years in, I became angry with myself, but turned to blame. Fifteen years in, I began to see he'd become complacent, so no longer trying. Thus, I became complacent and figured the thorn would remain since there was nothing I could really do about it.

In truth, the negative or evil foundation took hold of our relationship from even before the union of our marriage. It found the weakest spot and dug in until God was no longer present in our lives. Neither of us won. At the time, my husband gave into my inability to offer him what he also needed and desired in a relationship—marriage. The loss affected us a great deal in separate, negative ways, which ultimately ended the union.

Do not be foolish and assume evil, as stated in our Ephesians 5:16 verse, could never have any part of your day or your life. If this were the case, Paul would not have needed to forewarn the people of Ephesus. Rather, there would simply be two classes of people, the foolish and the wise. Unfortunately, even those who are wise in most areas of their lives can also be quite foolish in some others, which can bring them down quickly.

My ex-husband and I, equally, made some very poor, quite embarrassingly foolish decisions, leading to the demise of our marriage. What I found to not be coincidental, before it came to the final nail in the coffin, was the realization of our foolishness. I had the very clear thought to myself: "We can't go on living the next fifty years like this, essentially as friends, sometimes even enemies. Something has to give."

I sat for a moment and pondered the main thorn in my side. Then I considered what it would take to push through the pain to the other side of my healing. There was one area I managed to skirt around, in all of my therapy, because it was simply too painful, too raw to expose. I shuddered at the

Reclaimed

thought. I was being no different than Anne. Refusing to go to my intense, most vulnerable state. Fear had me in its vice-like grip, and I couldn't squeeze out of it.

What was I afraid of? The unknown? I had lived in a cage, which had kept me from getting too close to others intimately—for nearly my entire life. At least, ever since my hurtful grandfather crossed my boundaries. That specific action had basically told me that I had no right to think, feel, or desire anything, which wasn't *what others wanted* me to do. Because of this, I did not even know how to allow friends to know my true self since I didn't actually know who my true self was for so long. Even after marriage, I did not begin to really know who I was, until after I allowed God in to take control of my life.

I lived in this dysfunctional cage for nearly thirty years, and slowly, I truly began to heal other areas of my life. Step-by-step, I began to get comfortable with what was healthy, rather than cling to all the unhealthy I knew so well. However, in the matter of physical and emotional intimacy, I still remained caged by its sickness. The door was wide open. I could have willingly walked out at any time. Yet, what lay beyond the cage seemed so beyond my personal open comprehension. I truly feared what was considered "normal."

The downfall of our marriage dragged me out of the cage. In all honesty, by the roots of my hair, prac-

tically, screaming and kicking! Absolutely, the most pain I had ever felt in my entire life. I couldn't breathe. I couldn't think. The pain was debilitating, but I could no longer hide in the cage. Desperate to feel as normal as I could, I was trying to clean my house when a painful wave of my reality hit me and knocked me to my knees. "Help me Jesus," I whimpered and wept as I collapsed. It's all I was able to get out. And thankfully, it's all I needed. Once I managed to get back on my feet, I knew I needed to do whatever it took to save my marriage. Regardless of who was most at fault or in the wrong, I also knew the only person I could change was myself. I needed to face my cold, hard facts to ask myself the question I never felt I was obliged to own, "What do I want?"

What do I want? I remember thinking over this question for the longest time, knowing I needed to be honest with myself, or it would only get me nowhere, but back in the cage of dysfunction. "I want to feel desire, know desire, be desired," I finally answered. Might seem odd that a woman who had been sexually molested by her grandfather and raped twice as a teenager would come to this conclusion. The thing I did understand was that sexuality was a gift from God! I knew this as a fact. I had taught this to teens. A healthy, sexual relationship was essential in a marriage. And I wanted to be able to be vulnerable and honest to God's gift.

Simply acknowledging what I wanted was the first key to my freedom. I realized with this fact

Reclaimed

about myself, the cage had immediately disintegrated. Thus, I no longer even had the odd comfort of dysfunction to go back to. I now had to be true to myself. I'd found the thorn in my flesh, so I offered it to God to pluck out. His holy tweezers were poised, ready; I just needed to sit still, trust in His precision, as He easily removed it from my flesh.

"The tragedy of life is not that it ends so soon, but that we wait so long to begin it."

W. M. Lewis

Being outside of the cage was like knowing what it felt to really be alive for the first time. I looked around at the world, at my family, my children, my friends, and all I had embraced up to this point. And finally able to own it as mine, not just something expected of me, I had to do. For a while, I asked myself daily, "What do I want?" just to make sure I was answering for myself, and not out of fear or lack of boundaries to those around me.

My greatest gift was that I began to change within, learning to embrace and not fear an emotional intimacy with my husband. We worked slowly toward the physical intimacy. Setting up healthy boundaries amazed me as I never felt I had the right to own before. And some of them were specifically within my marriage. I no longer saw our issues as "all my fault." There were two who created

the marriage, which meant two pasts, two personalities, two beings who had their own ugly. I wanted to achieve an emotional intimacy; however, the damage had been done for us. Very important for me to explain to myself, for my healing purposes—if I could not feel emotionally safe, then I could not achieve safety in physical intimacy. When a union wasn't based on emotional intimacy, it was difficult to create as so much had eroded the trust, from both of our actions. I had to ask myself "What do I want?" and I needed to be true to myself. My response: "I want to be emotionally whole, dignified, respected, and truly happy."

Along the way, I heard from Anne again. She had broken through and confided in her husband what had happened to her as a young girl in the confines of her home. She also talked about it in therapy, too. When I asked what led her to finally speak, she said she was contacted by the family member's daughter. He was abusing her, and she called to confide in Anne. The reality of this type of evil, rarely staying with one victim, hit Anne deeply. She admitted to the guilt and shame she felt for not speaking out sooner, which might have kept this young woman from being a victim. However, she also knew she now needed to come forward to stop any further evil from spreading.

Four years later, Anne has continued on her healing journey. She's put the shame and guilt where it belonged, on her abuser, and she's healed even more by assisting others to heal. She created a program to gather items needed at a local shelter, which helps abuse survivors through recovery. When we Skyped, I saw a genuine smile on her face. It had not been easy, but one comment she made I can attest to, "I don't want to ever go back to living in that darkness. I want to live my life fully."

    I can proudly say I, too, have remained outside of the cage that kept me from experiencing the true gift in intimacy. Though I no longer get triggered, not necessarily the physical, yet more importantly not the emotional intimacy. I can trust. I can live. I can love.

REFLECTION ON HEALING

What do you want? I know, this is a hard question. When I get asked this, I hesitate because I think, "Do I have a right to say what I want?" Do you feel the same hesitation? It is normal. And it is okay to ask yourself this question and answer honestly. What do I want?

What do you want in your relationship(s)? Relationships take time and energy. When we are able to recognize the value and benefit of each relationship, we find ourselves with a much healthier balance in mood. We miss out on good, healthy relationships when we fail to admit what it is that we need, desire, and want. It's okay to realize that one relationship may not be offering what you want in all areas, or maybe it is in some. This is for you to decide. If one relationship is not serving your needs/desires/wants in any realm, maybe it's time to set a healthy boundary and not give so much energy or time to that relationship.

What do you want in your career? Whether you are in the workforce and/or raising a beautiful family, is it where you want it at this time? Are you comfortable, happy, content, exhilarated, challenged, successful, accomplished, at peace? This is different for everyone. What I may desire in what I do on a daily basis with my day-to-day interactions and with my family could be very different from what you or someone else desires. It doesn't matter what I or anyone else wants, this is about being *intentional* about what *you* want.

What do you want in your faith life? This may be the hardest question. Faith doesn't come easy, as it implies trust. And trust is hard for anyone regardless of the amount or type of trauma experienced. However, many long for the peace faith provides. This is about deciding what type of relationship you desire or long to have with God.

Take time to really ponder these questions. You may know right off the bat, or it could be the first time you've ever considered what you want because no one has ever asked you this question before. If "I don't know" comes to mind, then take a breather. You *do* know. Chances are you are still hesitant because it may feel selfish to acknowledge your own wants and desires.

seven | you've got this

"Therefore, do not continue in ignorance but try to understand what is the will of the Lord."

Ephesians 5:17

The will of the Lord. What *is* the will of the Lord?

"Rejoice always. Pray without ceasing. In all circumstances give thanks, for this is the will of God for you in Christ Jesus."

1 Thessalonians 5:16

Rejoice! Pray! Give thanks! Ha. Really? Is it so simple? How can we get to a place where we rejoice, even in the darkest times? How can we pray when we are angry at our circumstances? How can we give thanks when we don't feel thankful?

I've heard it said, "If it's in His will, then it will be." What does that mean? Especially when some would also allow it to be an argument for "why does God allow bad things to happen to me?"

We will never know, or embrace the will of the Lord, unless we *are* allowing Him to guide our lives. In Ephesians 5:17, we hear the words again: "try" along with "understand."

Once again, we are asked to do our best to trust God. To unfold in the will of the Lord is to trust in the direction He takes us. Take a moment and look back on your life. Think about when you were only ten years old. If you were asked at ten where would you be in twenty, thirty, forty, or fifty or more years, would you put yourself where you are today? Most likely not.

I know many things happened to me when I was in my teens, or even in my early twenties, I probably could have predicted. However, once I gave my life over to God in my late twenties, the world began to unfold before me in a way I never knew could have existed. So many opportunities were presented to me that I wanted to run from. But in prayer, and often because they seemed to show themselves in ways that were too hard to ignore, I trusted in what God was doing. I found myself introduced to gifts and talents I never knew existed within me.

Speaking in public, like most people, was a phobia I had in high school, even though I longed to be on a stage and act. I took four years of drama and never once auditioned for a play. Too afraid of failing, being judged, or ridiculed, for I believed myself *not good enough.* Empty arguments can keep you from your talents and dreams, too! But one of the first things God led me to do was to teach teens in Sunday school. Not just young teenagers, but eleventh and twelfth graders! They were closest to my age and, I feared, the most opinionated. Plus, I was not confident in what I knew about God, given that I'd lived through my worst days as a teenager myself and barely paid attention in church. How in the world could *I speak* in front of these thirty-five teenagers about something I'd only begun to embrace and learn about myself?

But I could not deny the fact that He had led me to do this, so I obliged. When it came time to give my first lesson, I prayed, asking God what He wanted me to do. In my heart, I heard, "Be genuine and authentic."

What did it mean? I agonized over this for nearly the entire week before the lesson. Then, after going through the lesson once again, I thought about a situation I'd recently been through in losing a friend of mine to suicide. The loss of his life broke my heart, and the means in which he did it made me feel so ashamed for not having been there for him more. During the week that I planned this first lesson, I'd spoken with my friend's mom. She told me about his struggles through high school and college, which I had not known about. Actually, he'd been diagnosed with bipolar disorder. Many life changes had happened at once for him, and apparently, he felt suicide his only way out. My heart ached when considering his presumed hopeless reality. Of course, unfortunately, his decision was too swift for me to even know about, and I found myself wishing he'd cried out to God instead. He truly had so much more life to live.

I thought about the teens in my class. I didn't know them. I didn't know their parents or their circumstances, but I knew I wanted them to know God was with them, always. I wanted them to know they could cry out to Him, rather than do something to harm themselves. This was the message I wanted to convey as genuinely and authentically as I could.

For the first time, I got up in front of those teens, with my nerves frazzled, and the sticky sweat of fear beading at my armpits. I spoke out and told them my friend's story. I was genuine in my reaction to his death, and authentic in my own misunderstanding of his entire situation. I led into God's teaching and what it meant to me. I prayed it would speak to them in whatever way God needed them to receive it all.

To my relief, the response was overwhelming. It allowed the door to be opened for the teens to feel comfortable, to even discuss their own circumstances with my older co-teacher and me. I learned that day that whatever made me angry, sad, hurt, disappointed, betrayed, happy, and joyful, often also made others feel the very same way. The more I spoke, and later began to write, with gut-wrenching truth, the more it led others

to come forward. They wanted to know how I had managed to find my joy and happiness.

Amazingly, just eighteen years ago, so if I were to ask myself where I'd be at the age of forty-six, I'd not have been able to even consider it all. I've received so many blessings and opportunities God's given me since then. Not to mention speaking internationally and to crowds over ten thousand! Who knew? God, of course!

When you recognize God's will as the most joyful and fulfilling path you can take, your life can be fully authentic. Granted, as I've stated earlier, no one is perfect. (But God still loves us unconditionally, in all our imperfections.) If it were up to God, it would be easy to recognize His plan, to receive it, and to follow it. But God wants us to *want* to follow Him. He doesn't want us to love Him, or follow Him because He *makes* us do so. Would you? Would you want your spouse to love you only because you said they *had* to? Would you want your friends to be your friends because you *made* them? Absolutely not!

God gave us free will in an effort to give us the *freedom and choice* to believe, and *trust* in Him, as well His plan, for our own benefit. And He once also gave free will to a certain angel, who decided he wanted to be more powerful than God. Yet, even God couldn't send this creature He loved desperately away. Rather, He sent him to his own space, devoid of God's light and life. Yes, some call this angel the devil, evil, or the enemy.

Reclaimed

"But by the envy of the devil, death entered the world, and they who are allied with him experience it."

Wisdom 2:24

Because he/it is mentioned in Ephesians as evil, I will refer to it/him as such. Evil wanted desperately to be perfect like God, and *still* desires this perfection. And evil believed the only way to reach this perceived perfection was to turn God's beloved—every single one of us—away from God. When I think about this, I get a pang of empathy toward this once gorgeous, ethereal creature. Evil's existence is devoid of life, so evil is desperate to take ours.

If we did not acknowledge the reality of evil in the world, then we would be ignorant. The Lord is asking us to be vigilant, but not fearful. If we seek and follow His will, then we have nothing to fear. But we are human, in an imperfect world, so there's probably moments we stray from God's will.

"Rejoice always. Pray without ceasing. In all circumstances give thanks, for this is the will of God for you in Christ Jesus. Do not quench the spirit. Do not despise prophetic utterances. Test everything; retain what is good. Refrain from every kind of evil."

1 Thessalonians 5:16-22

I began speaking and touring in my thirties. In the beginning, both terrified and exhilarated, as my phobia was not completely cured. I also still had many empty arguments swirling in my mind, threatening to quench my spirit. Often, I was with a team of other, more experienced, well-known speakers. From my leftover insecurities, I often compared myself to them, which led to a greater hesitancy. When I received my first standing ovation in front of five-thousand people, I broke out into tears. I didn't know how to receive it, and I definitely gave the glory to God, as I was humbled. He would use me to help others, and the mere fact I was given this gracious opportunity did overwhelm me. Each time after an event, I left high on the Holy Spirit. Honestly, it was an amazing experience, one I wanted more and more to know.

Some insecurity remained, and even with the accomplishments, it nagged and threatened my ability. I'd listen to the other speakers, and began to judge them versus how I'd have delivered their message. Like a thief in the night, my insecurity turned into envy. Instead of focusing solely on what message the Lord wanted me to deliver, I became more concerned about how I could deliver it like the others. Thus, forgoing the gift God had given to me, I wanted what they had instead. I can't say I realized I was no longer seeking the will of the Lord, because I was still speaking *for* Him. However, instead of each event ending with an exhilaration

Reclaimed

of being filled with the Holy Spirit, I left questioning everything I had said. It was as if I'd just heard the list of empty arguments shouting in my head at me.

My vigilance against evil had waned, and it snuck in ever so stealthily. Yet God is everywhere, and especially prior to one particular event which took place in Spokane, Washington. From Texas, I flew to Seattle, Washington, and then got onto a much smaller plane to Spokane. Seated close to the front, in the second row aisle seat, a young gentleman with tatted arms, buzzed-blond hair, brilliant blue eyes, sat next to me in the window seat. We acknowledged one another with a head nod, before we both settled into our own spaces. This plane was to land only a few hours before the conference was to begin. I knew I'd be cutting it close, so I focused on giving my keynote and the breakout sessions. I wanted to make sure I was prepared with the correct message.

Fifteen minutes into the flight, I gazed across the young man's shoulder through the window, seeing the mountainous peaks below us. My shoulder was lightly brushed by someone rushing by. Looking down the aisle, I saw the flight attendant, her face covered with sheer terror. She pulled her seat down and buckled herself in.

The smell of smoke filled the cabin. I turned to see other passengers moving from the back into empty seats up front. "Ladies and gentlemen," the

PA system crackled, "this is your pilot. Please stay in your seats and have your seatbelts fastened. We have a situation with the aircraft, and need to turn back immediately. Thank you."

The young man next me grabbed my arm, and I recognized the fear I was feeling on his face as well. "It's going to be okay," I reassured him, even though I wasn't so sure what was going to happen. This stranger and I held hands, while I leaned back in my seat, to pray. I prayed for my boys, my family and I thanked God for all He had done for me. "If this is to be, please don't let me suffer." I felt a peace wash over me, like a cool breeze on a hot summer day. The fear instantly gone, as I felt God with me.

An excruciating ten minutes later, we landed safely back in Seattle, with a dozen fire trucks and ambulances awaiting our arrival on the tarmac. We exited the plane and were bussed to the terminal where we were told they would work with us to get on another flight. The young man, whose name I still didn't know, or anything else about him, stuck close to my side. My peace soon got replaced by an amazing amount of adrenaline. Now, I was hesitant to get on another plane.

The young man turned to me and said, "Want to rent a car and drive to Spokane? I know how to get there. I've driven it several times." I hesitated, unsure I should be riding in a car with a complete stranger for four hours, but then we had just faced the fear of death together. What more could happen? I learned the young man's name, Ryan, my oldest son's name. Plus, he was a marine coming home from a tour in Afghanistan. He'd not seen his family in over a year.

So, we rented a car. For four hours, Ryan and I talked about life. A whopping twenty-three years old, he'd already suffered through many hardships. We never touched the radio. In those four hours, we came to know one another and discussed God's hand in our situation. When we got to Spokane, he asked me if I would meet his family. I knew the conference had already begun but, almost like an older sister, I felt I couldn't let Ryan down. He wanted to introduce me, a stranger, to his family. I met with them for about an hour, then he took me to the conference hall, where I was met by one of the priests, a fellow speaker and good friend. Something in seeing him made my resolve break, and I broke down in tears.

What I had planned to speak on was out the window, replaced by what God had blessed me with on the plane, then in the car ride. I didn't care what the other speakers thought, I only cared about sharing the message God had given me. My soul was awakened on the plane ride. In my moment of peace, whether I was to die or to live, I realized I'd lost track of God's will somewhere. And I knew I needed to get it back. I took a break from my particular speaking team after the awakening incident. I needed to reconnect with where God needed me to be, and to embrace again my own gifts, not seek the accolades of others.

"It all happens for a reason," some might say, though this statement is not the same as understanding the will of the Lord. I don't believe what happened on the plane necessarily happened for a reason, just like I don't believe God *made* my grandfather so succumbed with evil that he'd molest young girls. Or that God *made* the young men rape me in high school and college. No. I don't believe *their* free will choices were taken over by evil. No. God does not *make* things happen for a reason. Rather, God brings a *greater good* from every single situation, even accidents, diseases, and health scares, if we allow Him.

I flew home from Washington at the end of the weekend, on a plane, over Mt. Rainier, and instead of fear, I felt my same peace. The greater good God gave me in having the amazing opportunity I didn't pass up—to speak to Ryan. I know I helped him reconnect with who he was in God, and then to wake me up from my own slippery downfall.

REFLECTION ON HEALING

Sometimes it is difficult to know what to pray, especially when we feel so far removed from our faith or knowing God. Below is a prayer that I have often turned to, especially when I feel weak and insignificant in my circumstance.

> *"My Lord, God, I have no idea where I am going. I do not see the road ahead of me. I cannot know for certain where it will end. Nor do I really know myself, and the fact that I think that I am following your will does not mean that I am actually doing so. But I believe that the desire to please you does in fact please you. And I hope I have that desire in all that I am doing. I hope that I will never do anything apart from that desire. And I know that if I do this you will lead me by the right road though I may know nothing about it. Therefore I will trust you always though I may seem to be lost and in the shadow of death. I will not fear, for you are ever with me, and you will never leave me to face my perils alone. In Jesus Christ I pray. Amen"*

Thomas Merton, *Thoughts in Solitude*

eight | stand firm

"And do not get drunk on wine, which lies debauchery, but be filled with the Spirit."

Ephesians 5:18

I love wine. I appreciate its aroma, the boldness of the grape, the way varietals of wine can make the taste of chocolate or a good steak burst with new delicious flavors. I enjoy tasting new wines, visiting our local Texas wineries, and when the opportunity arises, to visit the Sonoma and Napa regions. This would *not* be considered debauchery. On the other hand, drinking a few bottles a night in an effort to drown our sorrows *is* dipping into debauchery, which is "excessive indulgence in sensual pleasures."

This verse can be considered difficult to ingest. I am not ashamed to admit I have fallen many times against this directive, especially when I wanted to be in control. Which is ironic, because when we fall into debauchery, we are typically the furthest from control.

It's a common response for survivors who've been controlled mentally and or physically. They sometimes overcompensate for the rest of their lives by trying to find ways to be in control of their feelings, pain, looks, emotions, and so forth. Often, this can lead to self-destructive behaviors, such as cutting, eating disorders, or addictions such as alcohol, drugs, or pain medications. They may even have an unhealthy cycle of depression and dependency—letting the pill bring them "up" without putting forth any real work to overcome the depression. The healthiest control we have is to not allow ourselves to be "controlled" by these behaviors, disorders, and addictions. We can do this by setting healthy boundaries in all of our relationships, and with ourselves personally.

What are boundaries? Boundaries are the lines we draw. It is the line where we say, "that is enough;" "you cannot do that;" "stop!" A boundary is a line you draw around yourself, which permits only the behaviors of others who are acceptable to you. Boundaries are necessary steps in self-care and self-development. Without boundaries, we are virtually powerless. We give away our personal power to the whims, desires and demands of others in our lives. Without our boundaries, we become or remain victims. [2]

---

[2] This information on boundaries was taken from an excerpt written by Pamela Grant in *Life Callings*

You cannot get your needs met if you are not willing to set significant boundaries for yourself. When you set a boundary, you are protecting your heart and soul, so keeping the empty arguments at bay.

In previous chapters, I've mentioned establishing boundaries. I've even given examples of others and the boundaries they have set. We are each unique individuals with our own stories and circumstances. Your boundaries will not be the same as the ones I have set for myself. We might have some in common, and I do believe there are some boundaries we can all benefit from setting, such as:

- No one may shame or guilt me in any way.
- I will not be pushed around.
- No one has the right to demean me.

When you begin to design your own boundaries, remember you are looking for the statement that gives you more than enough space to be your very best. For example:

- No one can force me to do something I don't want to do.
- When I give respect to others, I expect the same respect.
- I will not allow someone to yell or scream at me.

Reclaimed

Personal, internal boundaries could be something like this:

- I will not allow myself to lose awareness by (fill in the blank)—drinking more than two glasses of wine in one night, taking more pills than prescribed, or after the prescribed time.
- I will not purposefully cause harm to my body.
- I will make sure I eat the proper amount daily to keep my body nourished.

We all have our vices, and it is important to be truthful with what they are. For me, I'll be transparent and admit I struggle with stress eating and drinking. In March 2017, I had my thyroid, twelve lymph nodes, and a parathyroid removed due to metastatic papillary thyroid cancer. I received radiation in May 2017, and came out of the four-day isolation bloated, weighing nearly fifteen pounds heavier than I did going in. Granted, this was from the radiation as I had to ingest the radiation and be in isolation for three days. But my weight has always been a means of control for me. To have it completely skyrocket out of my control was devastating.

I worked diligently to eat the way I needed to eat, with only a synthetic thyroid drug to regulate my metabolism. I knew this would be more of a mental fight for me rather than physical because I happen to love food! But I also didn't want to go back to what I weighed in May. So, I chipped away at it, taking it one day at a time and doing fantastic. Then, at the end of August 2017, Hurricane Harvey hovered over Houston and dumped so much rain. Also, an area lake released more water, which led to our neighborhood, and many others in the Houston area, to be flooded. It was a rather surreal moment watching the gray water, filled with sewage and debris, rise up in my backyard, then slowly seep into my house. By the time we were rescued by boat, the water was up to my shins. In the midst of this hectic moment, I could only think about our family's safety.

The days that followed were chaotic, helping out at our church with other survivors who had no other family to stay with. Eventually, three days later, we were able to go back into our home, only to find everything soaked and contaminated. Watching the entire contents of my home being thrown out like trash on my front lawn was devastating. Yes, just stuff, but still it hurt me. We were all alive and well, a blessing we certainly didn't ignore.

I had no shoes, none. I walked out barefoot because we were wading in the waist-high water outside to get on the boat. I had no underwear. I failed to put any in my "go" bag. I had nothing but the shorts and top I wore to leave, and one pair of yoga pants with a t-shirt. We were at the mercy of our friends and family who didn't flood. Which

Reclaimed

meant we wore and ate what we were given—the best comfort food I'd ever indulged in. I didn't think twice about my weight.

For the next five months, as we re-nested from my in-laws to a friend's five-hundred-square-foot guest house, back to my in-laws, and then finally in the upstairs of our home. Still, I ate whatever I wanted, and we drank at least a few glasses of wine a night. I dropped any internal boundaries I had set because I convinced myself we deserved it. We were living through hell and comforting ourselves however we could.

Until, of course, the reality of the situation hit. This was going to take some time to get our home back in order. In reality, it would take almost a year from the date of the flood. I was desperate to get my life back into some semblance of normalcy, which meant I needed to reestablish my internal boundaries. I continue to struggle with my eating to this day. I have my internal boundaries on—what I know is healthy for me, what I can say yes to, when I can allow an indulgence in sparingly, and what is simply not acceptable. I try. I am not perfect, but I do try. I know there is always going to be one thing that will be my "thorn." But having lived through the ultimate pain, I also know I can and will conquer this as well. It's about trusting in the Lord and His directives—guidance.

Setting healthy boundaries with others also doesn't mean attacking the person or their character. Boundaries should be set lovingly and firmly. For example:

- "Sam, I don't like being yelled at. I want to hear what you have to say. Would you please lower your tone?"
- "Cathy, I have five minutes to talk with you. Will that work for you, or do you want to call me at another time?"
- "I am unable to be with you when you are angry. I love you, and want to spend time with you, but I need to leave the room now. I am willing to talk about this when you aren't upset."
- "I don't feel comfortable with these kinds of jokes. Please stop."

It doesn't matter what the other person's reaction is. The bottom line is you are standing up for yourself and letting the person know you are self-confident. Be direct and confident. Sometimes the person is so into their own empty arguments that they cannot hear you or won't respect your boundaries at all. In this case, you must state your boundaries in a strong and direct manner. Be firm:

- "Steve, that's it! You cannot yell at me ever again. Got it?"
- "That feels mean—stop it right now!"

Reclaimed

- "If you keep badgering me, I will not help you."
- "Kathy, I cannot hear one more word about how bad Tom is treating you."
- "Harry, you cannot be late any longer. The next time, you're fired."

When you feel the need to set a boundary, make the biggest request you can of the person to have them treat you exactly as *you* wish, and need to be treated. Do not try to figure out if they can do what you're asking. Just ask for it, or demand it if necessary. They may or may not be able to accept it and change their behavior accordingly. If they can, great! If they can't, it is not your problem. It is your problem, though, *if you compromise* your own self-esteem and self-integrity for the *acceptance* of someone else. If they give you a bad time or can't deliver, it is time to walk away. You must let them know you are serious and the consequences. Often, if you haven't set boundaries in your life, those boundaries will be tested. Hold the line. Your self-respect is at stake. Holding firm to your boundaries is a triumph of self-respect. People with self-respect are respected in all areas of their lives.

You must be willing to live with the consequences of your stand. Sometimes people are afraid of setting their boundaries for fear of losing someone, a business deal, or an opportunity. However, by not setting boundaries, you have already suffered consequences.

"...rather be filled with the Holy Spirit."

Eph. 5:18

Now, if you are determined to set your boundaries on alcohol, you do not allow yourself to be sucked into debauchery. This means not allowing the vice to bring you a false sense of control, completion, elation, joy, or happiness. You must be focused on what it feels like to be filled with the Holy Spirit. When I was younger and heard this statement, I'd roll my eyes, then picture Tammy Fay Baker, with her spider-like mascaraed eyelashes and caked-on makeup on the TV screen, declaring the power of the Holy Spirit. No, that's not it. Not at all.

To be filled with the Holy Spirit is to be embodied with *a pulsing certainty* of where you are, and that what you are doing is *right*. Then, you are right where you need to be, and where God desires you to be. Yes, there are moments when we can be overcome and feel a sense of euphoria, elation, or sheer joy, which is definitely a sign of the Holy Spirit, but this does not happen all the time.

One night, at a youth conference with my youth group, before I began speaking, I remember praying

Reclaimed

over my teens. I wanted them to clearly understand what it meant to have the gift of the Holy Spirit. My heart was desperate for them to have this gift that I had not known or received when I was their age. At the end of the evening, two men, a youth minister, and a chaperone for another youth group came over to me. One of them said, "I watched you pray over your group, and I have to say, I could literally see the Spirit working in you." He offered his hand to shake mine, and when I touched him, it was as if a spark had ignited inside of me. I began to giggle.

I managed a "thank you!" and went back to my teens, but I could not stop laughing. I had never, in my entire life, felt such a rapturous and complete joy. This went on for about thirty minutes, even as I tried to stifle the laughs to be serious, I simply could not stop. Finally, I calmed down, and had to explain to the group what happened.

I had received a true gift of the Holy Spirit, in such a literal way in the moment, I could not contain myself. Some receive it through the gift of tears, others simply sit quietly in their own dumbfounded silence as they enjoy the unexplained happiness. These moments, at least for me, are few and far between, but I know with certainty that the Holy Spirit is real. It desires for us to choose *Its* euphoria over the empty joys found in worldly addictions.

REFLECTION ON HEALING

What boundary suggestions resonate within you?

Is there someone in your life with whom you need to set a healthy boundary in regard to your communication or time spent together?

Sometimes a good, healthy boundary needs to be set within ourselves and how we speak about ourselves. Do you often comment with disappointment on your own weight, or your lack of intelligence/knowledge, or how you look in general? Besides God, the greatest love you'll ever have is of yourself. Setting a healthy boundary in how you speak about yourself immediately sets the tone for what you will allow others to say about you as well.

Work on one healthy boundary at a time. Stick to it. Don't falter. You are worth it. As these boundaries become set in the fabric of your life, you will notice less stress, less anxiety, less fear—because healthy boundaries bring healthy control of your life

An excellent book I recommend for further work on boundaries is:

Boundaries by John Townsend and Henry Cloud

Reclaimed

Awake My Soul - Survivor Prose

Only time, is this the answer? I honestly think so. I'm in a state of mind where I need to be alone. I mean emotionally. I need to guard what is sacred, not many understand. I'm not boasting, it just has to happen this way. I am in the process of being broken down. I must focus on The Truth, at least as I know it.

Something has happened. Clarity is coming into play. Thank you, Jesus. See, He is my very best friend. I cannot afford to even step a millimeter away. I'm maturing, as You want me to.
 I promise I won't give up. This walk hurts right now.

I feel Your hands around my heart. I am starting to see the whole picture. This isn't mine, it's yours, Father. I must admit, I'm way in love with you. Please give me the strength to hold on to this. My first love. My eternal love. Nothing will ever compare.

See, I am trying to help better my own understanding. This is it, Holly. All that you ever need is in my own hands, from You. I refuse to be hindered. Nothing can shake me. Your will Father. Your will. I really want to know You. I want to see Your face. I need You. I rely, depend, and will count on You. Forever and ever...Amen.

Holly, 42

nine | enjoy life!

"Address one another in psalms and hymns and spiritual songs, singing and playing to the Lord in your hearts."

Ephesians 5:19

God did not create us to live in the darkness, emotionally or physically. We were created with gifts, talents, desires, likes, and dislikes. God created us to enjoy all we love. It's time to focus and discover what you love. *Not* what your spouse or best friend loves, but what *you* love. Do you find pleasure in reading a book, taking a hike, getting a massage, traveling, or spending time with family and friends?

    I love to travel. At eleven, I went on my first trip on a plane alone to visit my cousin and her husband in Virginia. I was a little worried about being alone on the plane, but I knew my cousin would be there as soon as I disembarked. I was not going to miss the opportunity to see something new. It amazed me to drive around and see the pretty, varying landscapes. They were so vastly different from the flat and barren sites that surrounded me in north Texas. My cousin and her husband moved to Hawaii when I was thirteen, and once again, I managed to convince my parents she needed my help with the kids. Surrounded by colorful, tropical plants, aqua blue seas that looked as if a painted portrait, and sand as soft as plush carpet. Witnessing these variations of God's beauty became a true love of nature in my life.

By twenty-one, I'd traveled most of Germany and Denmark as a foreign exchange student. I turned down the opportunity to be an Oscar Meyer Weiner girl in the Weiner Mobile because it conflicted with my European trip to Italy, Austria, France, England, and Switzerland. Granted, I could have traveled the sites of the United States as an Oscar Meyer Weiner girl as well, but I figured I was young enough to still manage visiting most of the land of the brave before my time had come to get married or a career.

What would have been different if I had taken the job? I wonder this sometimes. I would have gone on to possibly pursue more of a career in marketing or public relations, which was my minor in college. Would I have married? Did I determine my life's course because I chose to stick with a plan to enjoy a little slice of life after graduation before having to enter the workforce?

The answer is nowhere to be found because it was not written in my life course. What did happen was that I took a job as a customer service representative for a clothing manufacturer that made Perry Ellis men's suits. I had an eight-state territory ranging from east Colorado across to Florida. Plus, the bonus of visiting New York four times a year for meetings. I loved travel, and I believe the Lord knew I harbored this love. The opportunities for me to see the world have been endless, and I am so grateful to God for offering them.

Focusing on the everyday loves is a bit more challenging, at least for me. The daily commitments as mother, wife, peer-support minister, and founder of a nonprofit left little time for me to consider what else I loved. Obviously, I adored my family and found great satisfaction in taking care of them and making sure I attended to their needs. Helping survivors to heal and walking alongside them on their recovery journey offered a deep, fulfilling gratification. Having found the courage, I pushed beyond my empty arguments, of not feeling good enough or worthy, and started up a 501 (c)(3) nonprofit. This aided in the long-term recovery for survivors of abuse, which exhilarated me in accomplishing.

Even still, I needed to allow myself a chance to embrace the smaller loves in my life, which helped to keep me positive and focused on the daily blessings. When we make a conscious effort to focus on the positive, then it isn't as hard to find ways in which God shows up for us on a daily basis. By enjoying the simple things, it's easier to handle the fallbacks or tough moments that occasionally emerge.

Music for instance, has been a calming sedative since my earliest memory. My Papa, my dad's father, the "good" grandfather, bought me a rocking chair. It had a small music box attached to its leg, so when you rocked back and forth, it would play a melody. Around three years old, I'd get up before the sun rose, everyone else in the house still nestled deep under the covers. I'd rock, with my thumb in my mouth, and favorite *"blankie"* up to my nose. Eventually, my body no longer fit in the miniature rocking chair, and I graduated to my dad's La-Z-Boy rocker. Up to my senior year in high school, I'd ache to rock in the chair, headphones on, and some favorites I listened to: George Michael, Madonna, Duran Duran, Depeche Mode, Poison, Janet Jackson, Michael Jackson, 2 Live Crew, Ice Cube, Naughty by Nature, Keith Whitley, George Straight, The Judds, Michael W. Smith and Amy Grant. I was certainly all over the place in music genres.

I connected with the emotions of the song lyrics and music. I let them carry me to another reality so I didn't have to face the pain of where I was in the moment. Music truly was an escape. Sitting in my rocking chair was an addiction. In college, I

was forced to let go of my need. But I learned to listen and embrace music on walks, or in the car, or even at night, as my roommate and I fell asleep. Music was still an escape, but I no longer needed to run from where I was. Music then allowed me to appreciate the moment I was in.

Now, music is a love I get to embrace on a daily basis. My taste is still all over the board, and I pick what I want to either enhance the mood I'm in, or help change my outlook. I remember the moment I realized I *had a choice* to help change my mood. Driving home from work, frustrated because I was hearing yet another horrible story of abuse, and my heart ached for this survivor. A song then came on that awakened the immediate desire to dance, and I started to change the station because I was not in the mood. *"Why not?"* I thought. *"Why allow myself to be brought down by this evil in the world? Why not celebrate the fact she talked and I listened?"* I rolled down my windows and cranked up the volume on the song. By the time I was home, my mood was lighter, I felt good about myself and my day.

Even as I sit and write this chapter, I see the sun peek through the clouds. I want to feel its warmth soak into my skin. So, I took a moment, went outside, laid on a bench, my skin receiving the rays like a sponge. It was only roughly eleven minutes, but it rejuvenated my spirit. Amazing what even a quick time-out can do for you.

Reclaimed

Celebrating simple moments in each day helps you to allow your heart to be open and to embrace others in a more grateful, loving way. Often, evil can stealthily seep in through how we choose to look at our circumstances. Remember, we can't change those around us, but we can choose how we react or respond to each moment we're given. When you choose to celebrate the small stuff, then the uncomfortable, frustrating, heartbreaking, and unmanageable can be easier to manage. Especially if you see it was not in your control.

When I was going through a very difficult time in my marriage, the overall mood was very heavy in our home. If given the opportunity, it would have crushed my spirit completely. But I was in the process of finding myself, recognizing what I wanted, and I came to the realization that I could either choose to be crushed, or choose to focus on my small celebrations instead for that day.

One particular day, during the same time, I was in my office, finished for the day and ready to go home in a good mood, but I was also wary of going home. I felt I'd be succumbed by the sadness that gripped our household. I sat back in my chair, thought about what I had accomplished at my work, proud of the fact I was even able to sit in my office, fully funded by my donors. They believed in what we were doing through Hopeful Hearts Ministry, so I chose to celebrate it. Suddenly, I had this real craving for a Daiquiri Ice, single-scoop cone

from Baskin Robbins. This might seem a bit juvenile to some, but it was as if I had to convince myself, *I had the right* to go and get an ice cream cone by myself. *I had never stopped to get ice cream alone.* I was either with my kids or, no, that's about it. I was always with my kids when I got ice cream. I had to laugh out loud to myself.

I went up the street to the ice cream shop, bought the cone, and drove the short distance back to my office. I sat on the couch eating my ice cream as if it were my last meal. Truly, I savored every single morsel of the cone, and when it was done, I looked around the room and smiled. There was a freedom in doing it by myself, even sitting in silence, enjoying a small piece of life alone and feeling joyful. It gave me hope. No matter what was to come in my life, the simple joys could not be taken away because I knew how to "be" and "enjoy" all on my own. True freedom.

"Now the Lord is the Spirit, and where the Spirit of the Lord is, there is freedom."

2 Corinthians 3:17

We are free to love ourselves, to enjoy ourselves, and to be comfortable with ourselves. Then we are able to address others with the same love, empathy, and care. Granted, there will always be sandpaper people in your life. You know, the ones who just

Reclaimed

rub you the wrong way, no matter how hard you try to like them? When you come across those people, you will have the ability to be gracious, and then kind enough to yourself to walk away from them.

"Address one another in psalms and hymns and spiritual songs, singing and playing to the Lord in your hearts."

Ephesians 5:19

In this verse, God wants us to address one another in psalms, hymns, and spiritual songs. Granted, I don't believe you'll ever find me addressing you with, "The Lord is my shepherd, there is nothing I shall want." (Psalm 23:1) Rather, what the Lord seeks is if we have learned to love ourselves, embrace the small celebrations and joys in the day, to show love for the Lord, and to trust Him. Then this will come out in our daily interactions with everyone we meet, even the sandpaper people.

We can only give what we have. If all you have inside is sadness, frustration, or even anger, then small remnants of this is given to everyone around you. But *now* you have depleted yourself of the empty arguments; you've set up healthy boundaries, and you've given permission to yourself—if you felt you needed it—to embrace the simplest of joys in each and every day. And, regardless if it is something someone else might not consider a joy, it only matters if you do.

We have one step left before you make your ultimate plan to move forward. This might be the most difficult, but trust me, it is the final step to being your true, authentic self.

REFLECTION ON HEALING

What are some of your simple joys in life? Try not to back down from this question. It can be just as uncomfortable as asking yourself what you want. Life is so busy that we fail to remember the little things that bring joy.

This is personal preference. For me, I enjoy getting a pedicure or massage. I also enjoy having the house to myself and reading a good book. For you, it could be going on a long run or walk. Maybe it's watching a movie or the shows you have on the DVR. For some, it could be whipping together a meal from a new recipe or working in the yard.

What could you do with the simple joys in life that would help you to celebrate those small victories of setting a boundary and holding to it? Or to celebrate overcoming a trigger or fear? Essentially, this is self-care. Recognizing those little victories took courage and internal strength. You deserve to celebrate! When we self-care, we are loving on ourselves, which brings about a happier, peaceful you. When you are happier and peaceful, then everyone else around you benefits from this new, positive energy.

ten | be thankful

"Giving thanks always and for everything, in the name of our Lord Jesus Christ to God the Father."

Ephesians 5:20

Are you thankful for your life? All of it? It isn't easy to do. How can we embrace the ugly and be thankful for having lived through it? *Forgiveness*. One of the most common setbacks to embrace your worth is giving and receiving forgiveness. And then, being thankful for your life—all of it.

Forgiveness is a touchy topic for many. I have sat in conferences and listened to what others said about forgiveness. Basically stating we *have to* forgive, we *have to* love others like the Lord does. We need to embrace them, whomever, and move forward. When I hear this, honestly, my skin crawls. Clearly, the person offering this message is insinuating forgiveness is so simple, so easy. I then know and truly feel that they have either never been a victim, or betrayed, or they are speaking from a surface facade. Saying what they believe you *should do almost instantly*.

True forgiveness of any kind is a journey. It takes a journey of the soul to forgive: all those who have harmed us; betrayed us; let us down; mistreated us, or failed to show us the compassion and mercy we deserve. This is why this is the last piece to the puzzle to freedom. Now, it is a truly simultaneous effort, because to forgive, we must be free from the negative empty arguments and able to embrace *self-love* and *self-respect*. When we care enough about ourselves, then we can acknowledge the true hurt and harm, which has been done to us by others. The real first step in forgiveness.

"Understanding is used too often as a convenient means to avoid and sidestep the process of acknowledging the hurts and wounds (which makes forgiving more effective). We cannot truly forgive until we admit that the offense is as wounding as it really is, and therefore really does need to be forgiven. When understanding becomes the substitute not only for forgiving, but for sharing about feelings, healing does not occur."

Charles Fink, As We Forgive Those

Growing up, I was taught to brush off any offense, forgive quickly, let it go. It confirmed the empty argument "my feelings didn't matter." Therefore, I *never* fully acknowledged how deep my wounds ran.

Shannon M. McGraw

When I went to my grandfather's memorial service, which *I chose* to go to because I needed to have my voice, to acknowledge out loud what he had done to me. He was cremated, and I knew I would be talking to space, but it was *my journey* to do so. It empowered me, and gave me the strength I needed, when I was ready, to fully forgive him.

To administer punishment to the "offender," there has to be a jailer. While it might feel like they are getting the deserved punishment by not forgiving, you are actually condemning yourself to the same sentence. Freedom comes only in forgiving the debt *created* by the offender. When we fail, or refuse to forgive, we are forever shackled in the same prison cell with the offender. My grandfather was already face-to-face with God, and I had *to trust* that God brought down whatever punishment He felt was required.

A few years later, when I went through the darkest time in my marriage, we both rightfully needed forgiveness. I then realized I was in need of mercy, and worthy to receive it, *merely because* I was a child of God, who died on the cross for my sins. Therefore, every single person around me was also given the same mercy, even my grandfather.

> *"God created mankind in His image; in the image of God He created them; male and female He created them."*
>
> *Genesis 1:27*

Reclaimed

God did not make a certain few in His image, He made both male and female in His image. Therefore, God will not pick out the few He loves enough to be forgiven. He forgives us all, yet it's up to us to seek forgiveness *and* embrace it fully.

"For God so loved the world that He gave His one and only Son, that whoever believes in Him shall not perish but have eternal life."

John 3:16

Whoever believes in Him shall not perish. We cannot know the hearts of those who hurt us, even if they have succumbed to evil. Up until the moment of meeting Christ at our deaths, I personally believe we have the opportunity to stand before Him and are given the opportunity to believe, as well repent. Even the most evil have one last chance.

If this is your first time to hear a concept of belief such as this, then I'm sure it is hard to swallow. I am not advocating to allow all of those in our lives, or all the evil people in the world, to run free from owning their actions. Not at all. If my grandfather were alive today, I would not be having dinner with him as if nothing had ever happened. And, neither do you have to have any future association with your attackers. I'm *not excusing* his evil behavior by forgiving him. Rather, I am *freeing myself* from the responsibility of what becomes of his soul, thus al-

lowing myself not just to survive, but *thrive*. What is to come of those who harm us is between them and God. What we do with *forgiveness is mercy*, and then turn control over to God.

I did the same for the young men who raped me in high school and in college. I don't wish to see them again, nor be friends with their families. But again, if I am to be forgiven for any wrong I have done in my life, then I needed to allow God to take my burden away from me. The shame they own was not mine to carry. The years I allowed the anger, rage, and betrayal to fester inside like poison seeped out as a multitude of empty arguments. They created a basket of shame I carried over my shoulder, forever obligated to what they'd done. When I chose to forgive, I laid the basket in Christ's hands as not mine to carry, and it freed me from their burden.

Not until I faced my own shame and guilt could my heart embrace the primal need to be forgiven. Forgiving myself, to receive God's forgiveness for what I knew was my sin and no one else's, happened to be the *most difficult step* for me in healing. Yes, easier to blame everything wrong in your life on someone else, or a situation, or unfortunate illness. These things cause great havoc and bring forth those empty arguments that lead us to paths we wish we'd never taken. However, we are still responsible for the choices we made and our reactions and responses to them.

Reclaimed

To be able to admit, *out loud and/or* on paper, I chose to do A. B. C., with a clear and conscious decision, which was humbling. Pride, for me, wanted to jump up and say, "Wait a minute, you did it because this happened to you?!" No, if I made pride sit down, I'd have to admit that I came to my decision knowing it was wrong and went ahead anyway. When you can come to a place where you can acknowledge what sin was in your life, you make pride sit down. With a repenting heart, seek forgiveness, then you'll know the true mercy of the Lord.

As a young girl, I imagined God to be like Mr. Clean in the sky. A big, bald, scary man who pointed His finger at me in disappointment. He then shunned me to a life of constant chaos and sadness. The moment I relented, asked God to take my life and *do something* with it, He revealed His true loving self to me. I no longer imagined Him in the sky, rather, He was right beside me on this journey, like a loving father, making sure I knew I was not alone. When alone in prayer, and in need of feeling accepted and appreciated, I picture Jesus. Yes, the way most movies or stories do, with the long brown hair and flowing white garment. Interestingly, He takes my hand to lead me in a waltz. I rest my face in the crook of His neck, as He guides me in the dance. There's a comfort in this, because I allowed Him to lead me, and it's effortless.

Now, my vision of God had changed when I went to seek forgiveness. I envisioned this loving father

who was grateful I came to Him. He was supportive and understanding. He made it easy for me to never want to fall into sin again.

Envisioning God as a loving father may be difficult for many who have not had a loving father in their lives. If this is something you struggle with, imagine the person in your life now who offers you the most love and acceptance. Even if you have to dig in your memory to pull up a vision of a teacher or even a stranger. At some point in your life, you've been shown mercy and it remains with you. Find your vision, and know God loved you through that individual.

"Give thanks to the Lord for He is good, His mercy endures forever."

Psalm 107:1

You are forgiven. You are freed. Your soul has awakened to more blessings and opportunities than you can imagine. Give thanks to the Lord for every aspect of your life, for by His mercy and grace you survived your past. Now, you can embrace your present and trust in God's will for your future.

REFLECTION ON HEALING

Who do you need to forgive in life? We all have someone who has hurt us in some way and often we "let it go," however, the pain of the hurt remains. We do this to ourselves as well. We make decisions that harm ourselves and we need to forgive ourselves. God is a forgiving God. The work is in acknowledging the pain, and *not* pushing it down or aside. The real forgiveness comes when we work on handing those whom we need to forgive over to God. Then trusting that, as much as we desire and deserve forgiveness, so does the person we need to forgive. And it would be between them—the person and God, their relationship. Now, you have unchained yourself.

Seek forgiveness for your sins while forgiving others for theirs.

Make your plan. With your facts in mind and boundaries in place, determine the reasonable changes you can integrate in your life. Always remember, one step at a time, to remove yourself from or change the circumstances that caused the empty arguments.

CELEBRATE the small moments, they make the biggest changes! No one trips over a mountain, it's always the pebbles.

Embrace *you*! Love yourself unconditionally! You are human, and God's child.

Always Give *thanks* to the Lord for everything around you!

acknowledgments

Reclaimed has been an inspiration within, from the moment God "woke me up" with the verses from Ephesians. I give honor to God. I am grateful to be honored, adored, dignified, and worthy in His name. However, without the willingness of the many women and men who have come through Hopeful Hearts Ministry for peer support, I would not have been able to utilize His blueprint for freedom.

Thank you to *the thrivers* who have allowed me to use their stories for examples, and to the thrivers who submitted their poetry and prose. Your expressions in words is a much-needed voice for so many who are on their healing journeys.

Alice Parker, wordsmith extraordinaire, you have been a godsend as an editor, mentor, and friend. God blessed me by putting us at the same table in our networking lunch. Nothing is ever a coincidence, but a true "God-incidence." Your direction, encouragement, and expertise have lifted me up and given wind to my clipped, mangled wings.

Jared Rosen, you truly are the *Book Whisperer*! Working with you was eye-opening and a true joy. Thank you for seeing the potential of what was here and making it what it needed to be to help so many. I am indebted to you.

To my proofreaders and encouraging critics: Morley Ware, Patricia Budd, and Steve Ackley. Without your love, care, and support, my confidence would not have shown through to finally get this book in print.

Angela Whitley, you have been my breath when I felt there was no way to breathe. You have reprimanded when I needed scolding, and you have encouraged when I needed someone to simply care. You have been Christ's light to my darkness, and I will forever love you, my friend.

To my sons Ryan and Seth, thank you for loving me, even when there were times you didn't like me. You are the greatest joy and blessing in my life.

Russell F. Carr, you are my blessing, my godsend. Your love, encouragement, and support are more than I could ever hope to receive.

Shannon M. McGraw

Finally, to my mom and all of my family and friends who have lifted me in prayer over the last six years and throughout my entire healing journey. Yes, it takes a village to raise a child, and it takes a tribe to keep one's spirit alive and motivated. Thank you for your love, care, and concern. I am eternally blessed and grateful.

about the author

Shannon McGraw was born in Wichita Falls, Texas and was raised in Sherman, Texas. She has an undergrad degree in journalism and public relations from the Stephen F. Austin State University, and a master's in fine arts from the University of Houston.

It's been said that the best thing about hitting bottom is, when we do, we have no place else to go but up. Such was the case with Shannon McGraw. At the age of twenty-seven, she found herself at the bottom of a life that was no longer tolerable. With no place to turn, she found faith and peace. Hers is a love story of trust, continuing to unfold day by day.

Shannon McGraw is a mental health peer-support specialist. Personally, she's an incest, rape, and cancer survivor, and also, the author of *Exposed* and *Redeemed*, and founder of Hopeful Hearts Ministry [501(c)(3)]. Shannon has spoken across the United

Reclaimed

States and internationally to thousands, addressing the realities and effects of abuse in our culture, sharing the graces faith provides for one's healing journey. She's been honored with the Family Time Women of Achievement Award for Women's Advocate in 2014, has been CBS Houston's featured author, and she's been a featured columnist with Choose-Now Ministries, *Lifestyle + Charity* magazine, and many more.

Shannon now travels worldwide, not only helping survivors of abuse, but men and women in all types of business to recognize their "*stuck points*" and to show up with intention! Her desire is to be a hopeful voice for all and encourage everyone regardless of age, gender, or race to overcome their past setbacks in an effort not just to survive, but to thrive.

www.ShannonMMcGraw.com
www.HopefulHeartsMinistry.org

www.ingramcontent.com/pod-product-compliance
Lightning Source LLC
LaVergne TN
LVHW041337080426
835512LV00006B/494